Walk Confidently
With God

For my dear friend, Matt

Walk Confidently With God

A Practical Guide to
Living a Debt-free, Stress-free Life

Patrick A. Brady

May you have the courage to

Trust God in All Things

Walk Confidently With God
A Practical Guide to Living a Debt-free, Stress-free Life
by Patrick A. Brady
www.walkconfidentlywithgod.com
www.patrickabrady.com

All biblical extracts have been taken from the New American Bible
(NAB).

Published by Manresa Publishing, Gambrills, Maryland

International Standard Book Number: 978-0-9842467-0-0

Printed in the United States of America

Cover design by Reni Tobin and AuthorSupport.com

Interior design by Williams Writing, Editing & Design

I dedicate this book to you, the reader.

I pray that God will use my words
as a beacon of hope and understanding
that will guide you down a path with Him—
a path that leads to true peace and joy.

Contents

Preface

When a couple falls in love and gets married, they do so with hopes and dreams of a wonderful life together. Regardless of what those dreams are, the reality of life is that dreams cost money. Two questions the couple must address are how badly to we want our dreams and how soon do we want them. Unfortunately, Americans live in a country that offers many tempting options to acquire our dreams sooner than later. In such an affluent nation which has steadily been shifting to a consumer-based economy, going into debt has become easier and easier. Even when times are good, a high personal debt is like a ticking time bomb for anyone.

With a high debt load, the loss of a job, a protracted illness, or the loss of a home from some type of natural disaster or the down-turn of the economy could prove to be devastating. The reality is that too many people are living from paycheck to paycheck. Some statistics show that the number one cause for divorce in this country is related to money. When couples are struggling to make ends meet or disagree on priorities for spending money, it is difficult to look beyond this stress to remember the reasons why they married in the first place. Certainly a prayer on many people's lips is "God help us."

It is precisely this prayer that has prompted me to

write this book. If God can help us, will He? Does He really answer our prayers? Is it really possible that God will actually help you personally survive financially difficult times? Is it really possible that God can help you improve your marriage? Is it really possible that God can help you find a job? Is it really possible for you to live completely debt-free? To all of these questions my answer is yes—if you will learn to trust Him.

In God We Trust

This simple yet profound phrase appears on all U.S. currency. Whether you are Christian, Jew, Muslim, or someone who in some way believes that there is a loving God who watches over the universe He created, ask yourself one simple question—Is it really God whom I trust or the money upon which this statement of faith is written?

Throughout scripture, we are called to trust God. In the Gospels, especially Luke, Jesus consistently tells His followers to trust God. A quick Internet search would reveal a plethora of articles and books expounding scripture verses again pointing out why we should trust God. However, I believe that it is not enough to know why you should trust God. For some, it isn't even enough to want to trust God. The challenge is learning how to actually trust Him. I submit to you that trust is something that takes time and experience to achieve. It can be developed with practice. In the following pages, I intend to share with you events in my life that led me to profound change in my relationship with God because I learned to truly trust Him.

Many of my friends have said they marvel at the life I

live and, quite honestly, so do I. To wake up every morning knowing you are loved by God, loved and admired by your wife and children, and are financially free to do whatever the Spirit calls you to do is truly a miracle. Living life every day with the confidence that you are not alone on this earth, knowing that God is by your side urging you on is an indescribable experience.

There are those who say that the good fortune we have experienced is the result of luck. While I will admit to having been mightily blessed, I am quite certain our good fortune has not been the result of random luck. Rather, it is because we have chosen to trust God in all aspects of our lives and, in doing so, we have been blessed spiritually, emotionally, physically, and even financially. I encourage you to read on for I write with the knowledge and confidence that God does not discriminate with His blessings. His promise to guide and bless His children is intended for all mankind and, therefore, *anyone* who trusts Him and follows the principles of which I write will be blessed. It is my prayer that in sharing my experiences and observations you, too, will know the joy and peace that comes from walking confidently with God.

Introduction

To some people, the very title of this book may seem like a contradiction in terms. *Walking with God*, whether confidently or not, certainly seems like it would indicate a spiritual book exploring the more ethereal aspects of life that one would find in the religious section of a bookstore. Yet, the subtitle refers to a practical guide to living debt-free and stress-free, which seems like a topic for either the financial section or self-help section of the store. Regardless of bookstore location, the two topics certainly appear to be mutually exclusive.

My experience over the past thirty years has led me to believe that quite the opposite is true, and it is for that reason I have decided to write this book. In the pages that follow I intend to share with you my journey that helped me discover how truly trusting God with every aspect of my life, especially my money, could change my life. I was a bitter man on the brink of divorce, a father who continually struggled to deal civilly with his young children, and someone buried in debt literally scraping to find enough money to feed his children. Through applying the principles I will describe in this book, I have become a man whose heart is at peace, happily married for thirty four years, a father with whom his grown children really like to spend time, and one who has been totally debt-free and financially independent for the past fifteen years.

I believe there is a significant difference between *knowledge* and *wisdom*. Knowledge is something that can be imparted through books, formal instruction (such as in a classroom), or informal instruction from someone with experience or expertise in a specific field. Wisdom, on the other hand, is gained through one's life experiences. It is when we humble ourselves enough to learn from the wisdom of those who've gone before us that we can avoid some of the pitfalls that come our way and can live an even fuller life. Too often we make things harder for ourselves because pride prevents us from turning to others to ask for help or advice.

I am writing this book to return the favors of these dear friends who have helped shape and change my life. It is my prayer that, in sharing the wisdom I have gained through my own experiences, you will also discover the richness of a life lived with and for God. And, perhaps, in time, you, too, will share your wisdom with those who come after you.

How to Read This Book

To help you best follow the path that led me to this discovery I have divided the book into three parts:

Part 1 is devoted to the story of my experiences through which I hope will help you see exciting possibilities for yourself regardless of your own personal circumstances.

Part 2 serves as the how-to section. In it, I provide detailed advice on how to assess your current financial situation and how to create and execute a plan to get out of debt. Because the method I teach really works, I also include in this section ways to handle your money once you've broken the cycle of living paycheck to paycheck and have increasingly more money left over every month.

Part 3 is the most important section of the book, for it addresses the spiritual aspect of my discovery and why I believe that, without God's help and guidance, the methods described in Part 2 will only yield partial results and whatever positive results are achieved will likely be short lived.

Caution

Because Part 2 may contain what you may consider the meat of the book, you may be tempted to gloss over the other sections to focus on the mechanics but that would be like a doctor immediately prescribing a treatment before carefully diagnosing the root cause of the symptoms. There are other capable resources available to help people better manage their finances, with some showing methods similar to what I describe in Part 2 to get out of debt. However, I assure you that being in debt is but a symptom, and getting out of debt is only the beginning of living what will be an awesome life.

To fully grasp the entire concept of walking confidently with God, I ask you to read the entire book. Once you've read the entire book, you will certainly want to study Part 2 as well as go to my website to make sure you master the mechanics of sound financial management. But before you do, be sure you take in the entire message.

PART 1

It Could Happen to You

Part 1 describes a significant time in my life — a time when I was desperately looking for help. While I certainly hope there is no one reading this book who is in as bad a place as I was, I tell this story to assure you that, regardless of your circumstances, there is nothing going on in your life that God can't or won't help you overcome. The purpose of telling this story is not just to give you hope but to show you some of the ways that will help you learn to trust God.

Among the many things I've learned over the past twenty years, one fact I know is that from both the positive side as well as the negative side of my story . . . it could happen to you.

1

Riches to Rags

Consider your ways! You have sown much, but have brought in little; you have eaten, but have not been satisfied; you have drunk, but have not been exhilarated; have clothed yourselves, but not been warmed; and he who earned wages earned them for a bag with holes in it.

HAGGAI 1:6

In January 1971, I was a senior in high school sitting in homeroom when my buddy, Dickie, suggested that we go talk to a Navy recruiter after school. Having lived in El Paso, TX most of my life, the idea of joining the Navy was certainly intriguing, especially to one who had never seen the ocean, let alone a Navy ship before. It seems that Dickie had been thinking about joining the Navy for quite some time and when we got to the recruiting station, his questions to the recruiter must have signaled that this fish was ready to bite, and he simply needed to reel him in.

Before I knew it, I was nodding up and down, discussing all the exciting possibilities of life in the Navy and filling out paperwork to bring home for my parents to sign allowing their seventeen-year-old son to join the Navy. My logic was quite simple really. First, joining the service would help me pay for college. With eight kids in the Brady family, the only way I was going to college was to pay for it myself.

While I had lots of scholarship possibilities, those that paid most or all of my expenses were football scholarships and having played serious Texas football since I was eight, I was burnt out and not at all interested in playing football in college. Joining the Navy, on the other hand, would entitle me to the GI Bill which would allow me to go to college and not play football.

Next, the idea of going to sea seemed awesome. It was a way of life totally foreign to me, and I was up for an adventure. And last, but certainly not least to a seventeen-year-old, I thought the Navy uniforms were so much cooler than the Army uniforms I was so used to seeing in El Paso. With six sisters, I saw first-hand how exited they got when they saw a guy in a sailor uniform.

Once in the Navy, I was given the opportunity to go to the U.S. Naval Academy in Annapolis, MD. This, too, seemed like a pretty simple decision. Going to the Academy would mean I would get my college degree, and once I graduated, I'd be an officer in charge of enlisted guys like me. When I found out that not only was the education free, but the Navy paid me to go, I simply said, "Where do I sign?"

After arriving at the Naval Academy and beginning plebe summer I thought I had died and gone to Hell! During my four years in Annapolis, I did not like the Academy at all, but what my parents and other adult friends were advising me was that, while the Naval Academy wasn't a good place to be *at*, it was a great place to be *from*. And since I would still have to resume my enlisted obligation to the Navy if I left the Academy, I decided to suck it up, and in 1976, graduated with an officer's commission and a BS in engineering.

During senior year, midshipmen are given the opportunity to choose which branch of the Navy they will enter after graduating. At that time, the officer I most admired was a man who was in the Surface Line community, the branch of the Navy where you spend most of your career aboard ship and ultimately become the captain of a ship. Therefore, I wanted to choose Surface Line, which also meant I had to choose my first ship (one that had an open billet that June after my graduation).

By that time I was engaged to Leslee, so my choice of ship was mostly dictated by what I thought was best for both of us. While my preference at the time was to be on the West Coast, I knew that Leslee was close to her family and felt that California was much too far away for her. Therefore I picked a ship in Mayport, FL so she could easily travel home to be with her family when I was at sea.

During my four years on sea duty, Leslee and I were separated about thirty eight months, so when it came time for shore duty I requested an assignment that had minimal stress and family separation, that would get us closer to Leslee's family, and that gave me the opportunity to explore the possibility of employment outside the Navy should I choose to resign my commission at the end of my initial five-year obligation. So with orders to teach at the Naval Academy, in September of 1980 Leslee and I moved to Maryland with our two-year-old son, Matthew, and our six-month-old daughter, Kathleen. And this is where my story begins and our troubles started.

I opened with this seemingly innocuous story of my early adulthood for a simple reason. Looking back, I can now see that the path I have traveled in life has been dictated by a series of choices I made at various points along the way. I've never had some grandiose plan for myself. I suspect, like most people, I simply wanted to be happy. If I am honest with myself, I think I've always felt that God was nudging me to do something for Him that in some way helped others. But beyond that, I think I just looked to the future with the hope of doing something fun and interesting, having a loving family, and living a life for which I could be proud.

As I examine the various choices I've made along the way I recognize that those choices were highly influenced by the people in my life at the time. Even as an adult, it always seemed to matter what others thought of me. Because other people's opinion of me mattered so much, in 1983 I found myself in a financially desperate situation. And it is at this point, we begin.

Perhaps you are reading this book because you are concerned with your current financial situation and are hoping to find a way to overcome your money challenges. Perhaps for the first time you are taking an honest look at your lifestyle and debt structure and are recognizing that if you were to lose your job, you are only three to six months away from financial ruin. While I believe it is never wise to be in debt, carrying a large debt places unnecessary pressure on you regarding the level of income required just to get by. The problem living in a country with an economy based on consumerism is that it promotes a mindset of making purchases based on monthly payments rather than total cost.

Consider the following questions:

- Are you in control of your finances?
    Do you know exactly how much money you make and exactly where you are spending that money?
- Are you living above your means?
    Do you spend more money than you make?
    Are you making payments on your credit cards or paying them off in full each month?
    Are you financing your car, vacation, furniture, major appliances, etc.?
- Is money affecting your relationship with your spouse and children?
    Do you argue with your spouse frequently about money?
    Do you get excessively angry with your kids because they want to buy things to keep up with fashion trends or the latest game craze?
    Is your spouse hesitant to speak with you about money for fear of a heated argument?
- Is money affecting your relationship with friends?

Do you feel envious of your friends at times over what seems to be a better lifestyle than yours? Do you avoid spending time with certain friends because, when you do, you feel embarrassed by what may feel like a difference in social status?

• Is money affecting your peace of mind?
Do you worry about money enough that you find it difficult to sleep at night?

• Is money affecting your self-image?
Does your financial situation make you feel in-adequate?
Do you get upset with yourself because you haven't done better financially?

• Is money affecting your relationship with God?
Do you find yourself upset with God because He doesn't seem to answer your prayer for help?

Twenty-five years ago I discovered that, because my answer to the first question, are you in control of your fi-nances, was *no*, my answer to the other six questions was absolutely *yes*. Yet, initially I was neither willing nor able to see how that was so. The reality is that most Americans, including our government, are choosing to live beyond their means. In a country where the government has a multi trillion dollar debt and a budget deficit in the trillions, the typical mindset today is to buy now and pay later.

The sad truth is that most people are living paycheck to paycheck because they are spending money they don't have to buy things they really don't need. The messages in advertising are consistent: *buy it now, no payments for three years, zero percent financing, you deserve the best*. While we are loath to point a finger at ourselves, I believe the root cause of unchecked consumerism is greed or selfishness.

So how did we get here? The fact is, the phenomenon of extensive consumer debt developed in the lifetime of the baby boomers (my generation). Our parents grew up in a culture that taught people to save their money and, once they could pay cash, only then did they make the purchase. The general purpose credit card was not widely used until I was out of college in the late seventies. Yet, today you can even charge your Big Mac at McDonalds! So as a member of the baby boomer generation, we should be asking ourselves how we made such a radical shift in our way of thinking.

To help answer this, I would like to share with you the part of my life story that ultimately led me to significant discoveries. These discoveries brought about amazing changes in my life without which I am quite certain I would have lost my family and everyone else and everything I hold dear. You see, I was one of those who rode the wave of that radical shift of thinking and, in 1983, I found myself at the brink of ruin.

By way of background, in 1980 my wife, Leslee, and I were often described by others as the cute young couple whom parents hoped their children would grow up to be like. I graduated from the Naval Academy in 1976 and Leslee from the University of Maryland and we married the fall after our graduations. After four years on sea duty home ported in Mayport, FL, I received orders to teach at the Naval Academy. We were excited about these orders because Leslee's family lived near Annapolis, and this would mean we would be surrounded by family and friends in a familiar setting.

Until this point we had either lived in apartments or base housing and were frugal with our money. So in September of 1980 when we drove up from Florida, we arrived at Leslee's parents' house a young couple with a two-year-old son and six-month-old daughter completely debt-free. I was a Navy lieutenant and Leslee was, by choice, a stay-at-home mom. We had the option to live in base housing which, at the Academy, is very nice. However, we thought that it was time for us to begin to establish our independence and, like others our age, chose to buy our first home.

While the homes we could afford were townhomes, we had our hearts set on purchasing a single family home because that would make a statement regarding our level of success in life. So we found a nice four bedroom rancher in the upper middle class suburb in which most of Leslee's family lived. When we applied for the loan, we easily qualified, but the monthly payments would make things tight. Our thinking was that I would be in line for promotion to lieutenant commander in a few years, so we could tighten our belts in the meantime. And this was important enough that, if necessary, Leslee could get a full-time job during that time so that we could make ends meet.

Some might remember that in 1980 the mortgage interest rates rose dramatically. Rates literally were going up as much as a point a month. This was also before the times when one could lock in a rate, so between the time we put in our contract and the time for settlement (which back then took two to three months) the interest rate on our loan went to 13%! I can still see the blood drain from Leslee's face when the loan officer calmly told us the new rate and monthly payment stating that "fortunately" we still qualified for the loan.

We may have qualified for the loan, but we certainly could not afford to make the payments, even with Leslee working full-time. So the prudent thing to do would have been to back out of the contract. But we were so emotionally determined to make this work that we got creative in finding a solution. After all, what would people think if we had to back out of the deal? We decided that if we could come up with the cash to assume the existing mortgage, we could keep the payments at the level we originally anticipated. The creativity came in coming up with $30,000 to assume the mortgage. To do so, we took a signature loan from the Navy Credit Union, I drew six months advance pay, and Leslee's parents and her grandparents secretly loaned us the balance.

So now that we had this new home (which we really couldn't afford) we needed to furnish it. Even after the hand-me-downs from various family members, the house was still pretty empty, so we took advantage of the great promotions at the local furniture stores promising delayed payments for six to twelve months.

Then after about six months of struggling to get the kids in and out of car seats in our two-door Chevy Blazer, we decided we needed a new car. So we sold our Blazer and VW bug to buy a four-door Honda Civic. We could have purchased a used 4-door sedan and not taken a loan, but we convinced ourselves that in the long run it was wiser to get a new car because there would be less maintenance costs.

In reality we were trying to look good in front of our family and friends. So we took a loan. Then we found that, with both of us working, we could not make do with one car, so we purchased yet another new car. After all, I was a Lieutenant in the Navy teaching at the Naval Academy. What would people think if I drove a clunker?

It was during this time that general purpose credit cards were becoming prominent. Not understanding how the system worked, I vividly remember how surprised I was when I received a solicitation in the mail for another credit card when I already had one. I asked Leslee if she thought it was a mistake because the letter said I was pre-approved, and I only needed to sign it and mail it in. Why didn't they know I already had a card? I was so naïve that I thought that there was only one BankAmericard (which was the predecessor of VISA and MasterCard). So I nervously signed the form and mailed it and, when I received my second card, I felt like we just received a pay raise!

Just three short years after moving from Florida to Maryland, we went from being completely debt free to a family buried in debt. We had a mortgage, two car loans, several consumer loans for furniture, appliances, and even a loan for a piano. And to make matters worse, we had five credit cards whose combined balances were close to $30,000!

I kept asking myself how this had happened. We didn't buy anything extravagant. We didn't take expensive vacations or drive luxury cars. I thought we were living our life just like our family, neighbors, and friends. So how did they do it? What I did not realize was that most of our family and friends were in debt like we were. But if I had been honest with myself back then, I would have had to admit that we ended up in that situation because we were simply spending money we didn't have. We were trying to keep up appearances. We were guilty of thinking we *deserved* to have things we couldn't afford. I think we believed that having those things would make us happy.

To those we spent time with, Leslee and I seemed like the ideal family. We had two adorable kids, we went to Mass every Sunday, were active in our parish, played on the church softball team, and were in a bowling league together. Older couples would often comment to us how wonderful it was to see the Brady family sitting in the front row every Sunday with our two little angels at our side. What no one knew was that behind closed doors, our life was a disaster. Our daily lives were completely controlled by money and the worry associated with the lack of it. The truth was that most Sundays we argued the entire car ride to church, and during Mass we were both thinking about how we would respond to the sharp retort the other had made just before coming through the church doors. And then as soon as we got back in the car, the arguments resumed.

Every morning when I looked into the mirror to shave, I was thinking about what a total loser I was — how I had completely failed as a husband and provider. I knew that my wife wanted to be a full-time mom but had to work because I couldn't hack it. In addition to a full-time job, Leslee was coaching, reffing, umping, and judging every kind of sporting event imaginable as long as they would pay her for her time. When I wasn't teaching at the Naval Academy, I was working on people's houses as a home improvement contractor. I also mowed lawns and would paint your fence or rake your leaves if you paid me.

And with all of that, we barely had enough to make the minimum payments on our credit cards. This lieutenant, who was on a fast track to making Admiral, was such a financial wreck that his wife's parents would have us over for dinner three to four nights a week so that their grandkids would not have to have pancakes or mac and cheese or peanut butter and jelly sandwiches for dinner. I think they were the only ones who suspected things might not be so great with us. Yet, quietly, they gave us help without criticism.

As you have probably surmised, this situation was taking its toll on our relationship. For many years friends and family have looked at me as a pretty straight arrow—someone who is serious about his relationship with God and the Catholic Church. Many would be quick to comment that Pat Brady is a really good guy, one who is kind and generous and loving. Well, the truth is, it is Leslee who people should admire, especially back then. I am a very emotional person, and I took my anxiety and remorse about our financial situation out on Leslee and the kids. I was certainly not physical in any way, but I was abusive verbally. Virtually all of the arguments we had were started by me. I was totally miserable and did my best to make my family miserable also.

To her credit, Leslee convinced me that we should seek marriage counseling, yet our situation had deteriorated to such an extent that our marriage counselor fired us! I will never forget the last session when our counselor told us that we should call it quits. She said that, while she rarely recommended it, she sincerely believed that she could see no hope for reconciliation. Leslee and I walked out of her office in stunned silence after being told we should go home and try our best to work out an amicable divorce settlement.

Whether it was a technique or not, we'll never know. But whatever it was, it certainly worked. After a completely silent ride home, we found ourselves sitting together on our living room sofa quietly pondering the words of our counselor. Finally, Leslee broke the silence, saying, "That lady is full of shit! We're not getting divorced. I don't want a divorce; I just want help fixing our problems." She then looked me straight in the eyes and said, "We took a vow for life, so what are we going to do to make this work?"

I have come to believe that my response to this direct question marked the beginning of an incredible journey for us both. I told Leslee that I really had no idea about what to do, but that the only thing I knew we should do was to fall on our face before God and ask for His help. And so for the first time in our married life, Leslee and I joined hands with truly sincere and open hearts and asked God to help save our marriage.

After this simple and straight-forward prayer, the two of us began to listen to each other with an earnest desire to understand. I called in sick the next day, and we spent the day together talking. By the end of the day, we began to remember how much we loved each other and why we chose to share our lives with each other. By taking an honest look at everything, we came to the simple conclusion that the basis for all our problems was money.

As a staunch cradle Catholic, I found myself embarrassed that I was so obsessed by money. I took pride in the fact that I was not a greedy person with ambitions of great wealth. In the Gospels, when Jesus cautions the disciples about the love of money being the root of all evil, I pridefully thought that those words were meant for others and not me. Yet, what I was forced to admit was that money was controlling everything in my daily life. The challenge I faced was, now that I recognized my problem, what could I do about it? It was at this point that God began to come to our aid.

2

God Help Us

As for you, do not seek what you are to eat and what you are to drink, and do not worry anymore.

LUKE 12:29

Less than a week after our prayer for help, I received a phone call from a complete stranger who had gotten my name off a bulletin board at the racquet club I belonged to. The gentleman said his name was John and explained that the pro at the club said I might be interested in playing racquetball. We met later that week to play and, when I came home, I couldn't wait to tell Leslee about my new friend.

Because I am by nature an introvert, I was surprised as to how open I was in my conversation with John during our time together on the court. I told Leslee that I felt like we were old friends and was very comfortable spending time with him. In a short period of time John and his wife, Shirley, became our best friends. I think what attracted us most to them was that they seemed to have a sense of peace about them as if they had nothing to be anxious about. We learned they were active fundamentalist Baptist Christians which, at times, from the outside must have seemed like a strange friendship with me being a conservative Catholic. But because of our friendship, I was open to what they had to say about life and their faith even though their strict adherence to the words of the Bible seemed foreign and at times uncomfortable to me.

As our friendship grew I gained the confidence to share with John the problems we were having financially and with our marriage. We obviously hid it well because John was genuinely shocked when I told him. What surprised me most was, unlike us, they really had no financial worries. My real shock came when I learned that they were debt-free, including their home. With that knowledge I had the courage to ask for John's help. Perhaps with his guidance we could get our finances under control.

While John agreed to help me, he also told me that he didn't think I was ready to hear the "truth." I was a bit put off by this statement and, when I asked why, he responded that the root of my problem was spiritual and not financial. I then threw up my guard, knowing that what was coming next was a fire and brimstone sermon filled with lots of quotes from the Bible. But in his wisdom and patience John did not force his opinion on me. He agreed to look at my debt structure and guide me as much as he could to help me attack my debt. However, he did warn me that without understanding and applying some Biblical principles, my efforts at best would be a band aid and would likely not succeed.

So we mapped out a plan for systematically attacking my debt which included finding ways to increase my income while reducing my spending. It also included finding ways to sell as many of my non-vital possessions as possible to apply to my debt. As an aside, the methods we used are sound financial principles and will be explained in detail later in this book.

As I went to work on executing the plan, I was focused and disciplined in my efforts, but after nine months of work, my debt remained the same. It seemed like every time I would make progress reducing my credit card debt, something would occur such as our washing machine dying, tires needing replacement, or airfare to attend to a funeral in the family, and we were right back where we started. My frustration mounted, and I began to feel a sense of desperation, so much that I decided to go back to John and actually listen to the sermon he had to have prepared for me.

To my surprise, that wasn't his plan. I told him that I was ready to listen, so "let me have it." Instead, he gave me a reading assignment. He asked me to read the books of Haggai and Malachi in the Old Testament. He could tell by the shocked look on my face that I would have much rather had a sermon. As a Catholic, I was not accustomed to reading the Bible. We were used to listening to Scripture being read at Mass and the priest explaining it to us. In fact, the last time I had actually read the Bible was in high school when we studied the Scriptures in religion class. As one who never missed Sunday Mass and frequently went to Mass during the week, I felt I got all the Bible I needed when it was read during Mass. In fact, I didn't even recognize the names of the books John asked me to read.

While I'm about to share with you what I learned, I encourage you to stop, find your Bible and read these two books yourself. Don't panic; they are two of the shortest books in the Old Testament, comprising only a few pages each, and you will find them at the very end of the Old Testament. I have learned that, no matter what I can tell you about what the words of the Bible say and mean, by reading them yourself you allow God to touch your heart in a way no one else can.

That evening after Leslee went to bed, I went into another room by myself to do my reading assignment. It took a while to find my Bible, which was the one issued to me as a plebe at the Naval Academy, and once I found it, I noticed a sense of nervous anticipation. So before I began to read, I asked God to open my eyes and my heart to His wisdom. I first read Haggai. God's message to his people was simple and repeated over and over again. "Consider your ways." The following is an excerpt to give you a sense of the written word:

> 5 *Now thus says the Lord of hosts: consider your ways!*
> 6 *You have sown much, but have brought in little; you have eaten, but have not been satisfied; you have drunk, but have not been exhilarated; have clothed yourselves, but not been warmed; and he who earned wages earned them for a bag with holes in it.* 7 *Thus says the Lord of hosts: consider your ways!* 8 *Go up into the hill country; bring timber, and build the house*

that I may take pleasure in it and receive my glory,
says the Lord. ⁹ *You expected much, but it comes to*
little; and what you brought home, I blew away. For
what cause says the Lord of hosts. Because my house
lies in ruins, while each of you hurries to his own
house. ¹⁰ *Therefore the heavens withheld from you*
their dew, and the earth her crops. ¹¹ *And I called*
for a drought upon the land and upon the mountains;
upon the grain, and upon the wine, and upon the oil,
and upon all that the ground brings forth; upon men
and upon beasts, and upon all that is produced by
hand. {Haggai 1:5-11}

The background to this book is interesting. The prophet
Haggai is writing to the Israelites not long after they've
returned to Jerusalem following their Babylonian captiv-
ity. Because the temple had been destroyed during the
Babylonian siege, the Israelites had the task of rebuilding
the temple, as they were also rebuilding their own homes.
For various reasons, there were some snags involved in
the construction of the temple, so over time, the Israelites
focused their attention on their own homes and stopped
worrying about the temple. So God's message through
Haggai is, "Hey! You guys are so busy working on your
own stuff, you've forgotten me!" Unlike other times when
the Israelites had backslid into idolatry and immoral living,
this time the beef God had with His people was that they
were so focused on the everyday things of life such as their
jobs, the kids, sports, yard work etc., they seemed to not
make time for God (sound familiar?). The temple still lay

in ruins. So God is saying to them, "If you're wondering why you're just getting by . . . consider your ways."

As I began to study this book more, I found that the coolest thing about this point in history was that not only did the Israelites not kill or mistreat the messenger, which they had a habit of doing, they actually responded to God's call. They refocused their attention and energies on getting the temple built and began to put God front and center in their lives, and immediately they began to flourish as a nation. All the snags surrounding the temple construction were worked out, their harvests were huge, and commerce in general was lucrative. Life became good for the Jews in Jerusalem!

Reading this felt like someone shining a spotlight on me. I felt a stirring in my gut like I had never felt before. I was so worried about our problems that emotionally as well as intellectually I pushed God aside. Perhaps my pride was also kicking in as I thought I got myself into this mess; I can get myself out of it! As a Catholic, I was dutiful. I never missed Mass, I prayed before meals and before bed, and even said my rosary at least once a week. But God was this big guy out there. Jesus was certainly not someone I would consider a brother or friend. I did things because that's what I was taught you did to be a *good Catholic,* and in doing so, I would go to Heaven. Yet, the words that kept resonating in my mind were "Consider your ways."

Yes, I loved God. But my relationship with Him was pretty abstract. I completely separated God from my real life. God was someone I turned to regarding sin, prayer, and Heavenly matters — matters of the soul. I thought God was way too busy and I was far too insignificant to bother him with trivial matters regarding my credit card debt. I began to think, is it possible that God was telling me I was wrong? Was he really saying that He wanted to help me, but would only do so if I asked?

Having finished with Haggai and beginning to feel a sense of hope, I anxiously moved on to Malachi. The name of this book is actually a pseudonym because the nature of the message was such that the writer did not want to catch the heat that he knew his words would bring. Malachi is actually Hebrew for messenger and his message was certainly not something the Hebrews wanted to hear, and frankly, 2,500 years later, neither did I.

Historically, the Hebrews whom Malachi is addressing are the grandchildren of the Hebrews Haggai called to task. Because of the blessings that poured out on their ancestors when they put God first in their lives, this generation of Hebrews inherited a pretty sweet gig. From the work, sacrifices, and faithfulness of those who preceded them, these Hebrews, living as free citizens of Jerusalem, were comfortable — so much so that they had forgotten why they were blessed.

Therefore, with regard to their relationship with God, they were just going through the motions. While they were making their obligatory sacrifices, they were using sick or deformed lambs instead of unblemished lambs; they prayed only when they were directed to pray and followed the Mosaic law strictly out of obligation. In general, they were just going through the motions, following the law with their head and not their heart—doing the minimum. Life was good, so they didn't see why they would need God.

As I have come to understand it, God's chosen people were so busy living the good life that they didn't even recognize that they were missing out on a great life, one that only comes from walking confidently with God. And so Malachi, our mysterious messenger of God, tells the Jews they are being cursed because they were robbing God.

> 7 *Since the days of your fathers you have turned aside from my statutes, and have not kept them. Return to me, and I will return to you, says the Lord of hosts. Yet you say, "How must we return?"* 8 *Dare a man rob God? Yet you are robbing me! And you say, "How do we rob you?" In tithes and in offerings!* 9 *You are indeed accursed, for you, the whole nation, rob me.* 10 *Bring the whole tithe into the storehouse, that there may be food in my house, and try me in this, says the Lord of hosts: shall I not open for you the floodgates of heaven, to pour down blessing upon you without measure? {Malachi 3:7-10}*

When I read these words my heart was in my throat. The emotions that welled up in me were those of anger, frustration and despair. I thought to myself, are you kidding? TITHING? This is what John was so surreptitiously leading me to do! I am so broke that I don't even have enough money after paying the minimum on all my bills to give my kids a decent meal every day, and this guy expects me to give10% of my money away!

Even though it was pretty late I picked up the phone and called John. From the sound of the groggy greeting, I'm sure I woke him. But I was too upset to care or apologize. I immediately began ranting, "I did the reading like you said, and I get the message, but there is no way I can do this. I've been straight with you about my situation, John. I don't have one dollar to spare. You're asking me to make a choice between feeding my kids and giving my money away. You cannot take the Bible literally. God gave us common sense, and common sense says that for me to tithe in the shape I'm in now is insane. Once I get out from under all this debt I'll be happy to help the needy. But my *family* is needy." The more I ranted, the more emotional I became, and by the end of my tirade, tears were streaming down my cheeks.

John never tried to interrupt me or get defensive in any way. He simply waited for me to finish. When I was out of steam, he told me how sorry he was that I was so upset. His voice was calm and his words were clearly meant with love. He never said a word about what I read or how to interpret or understand the words. John simply led me to yet another passage in the Bible. He asked me to hang up the phone and read Luke 12:23-34 and told me, if I was still upset and needed to talk, to please call him and he would come over.

And so I hung up and turned to the passage he suggested. When reading these words I finally began to *know*

Jesus and understand His message to us all. As I read I felt like a child sitting in the arms of his father after a bad dream listening to him reassure me that I was safe and that God would never let something bad happen to me.

Please open your heart and consider the words of Jesus as He spoke to His disciples:

> 22 *Therefore I tell you, do not worry about your life and what you will eat, or about your body and what you will wear.* 23 *For life is more than good and the body more than clothing.* 24 *Notice the ravens: they do not sow or reap; they have neither storehouse nor barn, yet God feeds them. How much more important are you than birds?* 25 *Can any of you by worrying add a moment to your life-span?* 26 *If even the smallest things are beyond your control, why are you anxious about the rest?* 27 *Notice how the flowers grow. They do not toil or spin. But I tell you, not even Solomon in all his splendor was dressed like one of them.* 28 *If God so clothes the grass in the field that grows today and is thrown into the oven tomorrow, will he not much more provide for you, O you of little faith?* 29 *As for you, do not seek what you are to eat and what you are to drink, and do not worry anymore.* 30 *All the nations of the world seek for these things and your Father knows that you need them.* 31 *Instead, seek his kingdom, and these other things will be given you besides.* 32 *Do not be afraid any longer, little flock, for your Father is pleased to give you the kingdom.* 33 *Sell your belongings and give alms. Provide money bags*

*for yourselves that do not wear out, an inexhaustible
treasure in heaven that no thief can reach nor moth
destroy.* 34 *For where your treasure is, there also will
your heart be. {Luke 12:22-34}*

When I read these words, a recent memory came
vividly to mind. My son, Matthew, was five years old at
the time and was a tiny child. He was easily a full head
shorter than all his peers. Just a few weeks earlier he and
I were at our neighborhood public swimming pool, and
Matt wanted me to help him go into the water. While all
his friends were in the shallow end having a grand time,
Matt stood on the side absolutely terrified to get in.

Even though the water was only three feet deep, it
came up to his chin and he knew that, because the water
was choppy from all the playing children, it would rise
to his nose or higher. In spite of his fear he desperately
wanted to get in the water, so he asked for my help. The
memory that was so clear in my mind was the image of me
standing waist-deep in the water and this terrified little toe
head standing on the edge of the pool shaking and crying. I
kept encouraging him to jump into my arms, telling him to
trust me, that I would not drop him or let anything happen
to him. He kept crying, "No, Papa, no. I'm afraid." After
several minutes with me standing at the edge of the pool,
he finally leapt to me, throwing his arms around my neck,
squeezing as tight as he possibly could. As soon as he was
in my arms I kept saying over and over again, "See, Matt?
I've got you. I won't let anything happen to you. I'm your
father, and I love you, and I won't let you go."

It was in these words I clearly heard God's voice. God was telling me, Trust Me, Pat, trust Me. I'm your father, and I love you, and I won't let you go." When I was in the pool, I was standing with sure footing in shallow water. I knew the environment in which I stood and knew that I had the ability to catch and protect my son. I realized then that it was the same for God. I was terrified because I was unsure of what would happen if I jumped. Yet, just as I promised Matt, if I just trusted my Father, He would not let me fall. If God created the world, took human form, cured the sick, raised people from the dead, and ultimately rose from the dead Himself, how minor a task it would be for Him to help me deal with my financial problems.

And with that realization I began to sob and, through my tears, I spoke to God as my Father. In the Lord's Prayer Jesus used the Aramaic word *Abba* when He taught us to address God. The closest English word to Abba would be Daddy, which is the loving term a child uses to address his father. That night God ceased to be the stern, white-haired man with a long white beard. God became my Dad.

I didn't need to call John back. I now knew that John was simply God's messenger pointing me to God. I just needed to trust God and trust Him completely with every aspect of my life. While all my problems still lay before me, I was overcome with a sense of calm. I no longer felt anxious or alone. I had no idea how my problems would be fixed; I only knew that, with God at my side, they would be fixed because *we* would work on them together.

I don't know how late it was, but when I did go to bed, I slept like a child who had fallen asleep in his father's arms after coming to him with a nightmare. In the morning when I awoke, I was relieved and excited. I began my day by truly thanking God that I was alive and that He was willing to help me find my way. I decided that the first step was to get to know Him better by reading the Bible and, to do so, I promised to read a portion of the Bible every day.

I knew that this would take time and that I would need guidance in learning to read Scripture, and that morning I wanted to be sure God knew that I got the message and really, really trusted Him. And so to literally leap into His arms, I promised God that morning that for the rest of my life the first 10% of every dollar I received/earned would go to Him and that I would share His message of love and trust to as many people as I could.

3

Prayers Answered

Try me in this says the Lord of hosts: shall I not open for you the floodgates of heaven, to pour down blessing upon you without measure.

MALACHI 3:10

The next day I talked to John about my revelation, and he recommended several books that would help me both in reading the Bible and in understanding the biblical principle of tithing. What happened over the next six months was so astounding that I run the risk of losing your trust in the veracity of my story. I assure you that what I share with you is neither fabricated nor exaggerated. I often wonder why God's blessings were so abundant with me, but I can only guess that God knew the brokenness of my heart, my total surrender to His will, and the sincerity in my actions, and rewarded me accordingly.

As I explained to John, we really were in the position of having to choose between food and tithing when I made my leap of faith. While I am about to share with you some of the highlights of the six months following my promise, I want you to know that, from the moment we began to tithe, never once did we go without food nor did I ever miss a monthly payment for any of our financial obligations. My initial plan was to show my trust by tithing while looking at every possible opportunity for making extra money. I remember telling myself, I'm young, I don't need much sleep. I thought I could take on at least one other job or maybe God would open the door for a higher paying job that could replace one of the part-time jobs I was already doing.

Because of a serious injury I sustained while fighting a fire in the engineering compartment of an aircraft carrier, the Navy doctors determined that I was unfit for sea duty. Consequently, I was allowed to transfer into the Navy Civil Engineer Corps, which is non-seagoing, with the caveat that my medical condition be monitored on a monthly basis. Two weeks after my promise to God, I was at my monthly doctor's appointment at Bethesda Naval Hospital, and the doctor explained that my condition was getting worse, and that it was time to convene a medical board to have me discharged from the Navy.

This came as a shock to me and, when I asked about the timing, it was explained that, because I had been followed by the doctors at Bethesda for two years, the process would take no more than six weeks. This meant that in six weeks I would be unemployed! As I was driving home my initial thought was, great, I just start tithing and, bam, I'm out of a job. Then I caught myself and began talking to God. My conversation was something like, "Well, Lord,

I have no idea what's up, but I trust you. Please help me recognize the opportunities you're sending my way."

The next day I gave the news to my boss, who was the Public Works Officer at the Naval Academy. My job within the Public Works Office was that of Special Projects Officer in which I was responsible for all the high visibility construction projects being planned for the next five to ten years. In this position I functioned quite independently, coordinating with architects, engineers, and general contractors overseeing existing projects while working with special committees regarding the planning and design of future facilities. So when the captain learned of my imminent departure, he felt that there was insufficient time to transfer another officer onto his staff, let alone bring him or her up to speed. Therefore, he called the Bureau of Medicine and discussed the matter with them.

The next day, the Public Works Officer called me into his office to explain that he had made arrangements to have me placed on limited duty status for a six-month medical evaluation period. While the doctors were already certain of my condition, this would buy us time. It was early June of 1984, and I would have until the end of the year to make the transition.

The deal I was given was to keep my projects going and turn the oversight of them over as soon as an individual was identified to take the lead and brought up to speed. The captain told me I had no restrictions to my daily activities and that if I could make things happen on a few hours a week, I was free to come and go as I pleased. He encouraged me to use that time to explore what career I would pursue after the Navy. I was, in fact, able to make the transition and turn my projects over quickly and efficiently, so much so that I easily had at least an extra thirty hours of time available every week.

As soon as my boss explained his plan, I figured I might even be able to find a full-time job that I could do while I was looking for a new career. But before I could even begin to look at the classifieds, another door flew open. The very next day I got a phone call from a man named Dan who had been at a cocktail party the night before during which he had a conversation with my boss. Dan invited me to lunch, saying that he wanted to discuss a possible opportunity for me. At lunch, Dan explained that he was in the initial stages of starting a company that did something called forensic engineering, and in his conversation with the Public Works Office, it was suggested that Dan speak with me. He told Dan that I was a man who could get things done.

In 1984 the concept of forensic engineering was at the visionary stage, and only a handful of engineers were even dabbling in it. I had never heard of it. When Dan explained that a forensic engineer looks at something that is broken, such as a collapsed building, a boiler explosion, even an automobile or plane crash and figures out how and why it happened, I realized that, in my last sea tour as an engineer on one of the Navy's oldest aircraft carriers, forensic engineering was something I did just about every day. Lawyers and insurance companies were hiring engineers with various expertise as consultants to advise them and possibly testify as expert witnesses in court. Dan's company, which he was calling Forensic Technologies International (FTI) was going to commercialize this concept by giving the potential client one phone number to call, and FTI would find the engineer with the appropriate credentials to do the work.

So we ended our lunch conversation with Dan inviting me to come over to his office, which was a tiny 1,000 square foot space just outside the gates of the Naval Academy, to see if there may be any "interesting" cases that I might want to be part of. It just so happened that, while we were at lunch, a lawyer called the office with a potential case that involved a ship that sank in the mouth of the Congo River. It was a high dollar lawsuit scheduled to go to trial in six months.

When reviewing the particulars of the case, I found the nature of the work was well within my experience, so I agreed to help manage a team of experts to examine the evidence and testify to our findings in court. When Dan suggested that he pay me $25/hr (in 1984 mind you) I could barely hide my excitement. As it turned out it, the work was quite involved and required thirty to forty hours a week of my time for six months.

Two weeks later, the Public Works Officer once again called me to his office to tell me that he had received a call from the Commander-in-Chief of the Navy Civil Engineer Corps asking for information about Pat Brady because apparently I had been deep selected for promotion to Lieutenant Commander. What that means is that, after a specified number of years at any given rank, an officer is then screened to be promoted to the next rank. During this screening process the selection board also reviews the records of the top officers in the year groups one to two years junior, to see if there are some hot shots they want to promote early.

And so just three weeks after my promise to tithe, I found myself promoted two years early, receiving pay as a Navy Lieutenant Commander, and simultaneously getting paid $25/hr for thirty to forty hours a week. Keeping my promise to God, during this time I was giving literally thousands of dollars away.

In addition to the consulting work, many other small things occurred, such as the Navy Finance Center, when clearing their books in anticipation of my discharge, found a computation error in my pay, resulting in a check for a couple thousand dollars that we hadn't anticipated. With so many amazing things happening in our life, I certainly had a compelling argument for the existence of God and so, like me, Leslee had no problem recognizing the Hand of God and accepting the practice of tithing.

As the year drew to a close, Leslee and I looked back at the previous six months and marveled at the changes in our lives. Approaching the end of my Navy Career, I was stepping into a new and exciting career in forensic engineering as an independent consultant. As a couple, our relationship had improved by leaps and bounds. Our sense of peace and confidence was almost indescribable. We had simplified and prioritized our lives and were no longer concerned with keeping up with our relatives and friends.

Through reading the Bible, I understood that God did not intend for anyone to live in a constant state of indebtedness. Therefore, with the guidance from John and other friends who were completely debt-free, we had a plan in place to completely eliminate our debt in five years. And by the end of 1984, just six months after my leap, we finished the first step by eliminating our huge credit card debt.

It is important that you understand that this was not a fluke or luck and certainly wasn't a one-time event. We have remained faithful to God for the past twenty-five years. In accordance with our five-year plan, by the end of 1986 we had paid off both our cars and all other consumer loans, leaving our mortgage as the only debt remaining. By 1990 we had enough money saved to pay off our home, and after five more years of putting money aside, in 1995 we wrote our final mortgage check with enough money in the bank to pay for college for all three of our children.

Today all of our children have graduated from college and are happily married. We have no residual debt from the kids' college education or weddings. Leslee and I live in a lovely home on eleven acres for which we paid cash, and it is located near all three of our children. We fixed it up in such a way that we call it a kid magnet to make sure our children and grandchildren always look forward to visiting us. We are a very close knit family, and I am so proud to see what awesome adults our children and their spouses have become. They love each other deeply, have a loving relationship with God, and are faithful to the teachings of scripture by living within their means and placing a premium on quality of life instead of succumbing to the allure of consumerism. And yes, they all tithe.

I tell you this not to brag, but to give you hope. We accomplished this without winning the lottery or inheriting a large sum of money from a distant relative or receiving any other type of financial windfall. Instead, it took discipline to deny the seduction of modern consumerism and to live within our means. It took a willingness to work hard and a submissive attitude to follow the advice of others who led by example. And more than anything else, it took a humble recognition that all we have is a gift from God who simply asks us to be good stewards of His gifts.

God wants you to be happy. He created you to be His companion, not His servant. Yet in His great love for us, we were given the freedom to accept or reject His love, guidance, and blessings. God simply asks us to trust Him. Trust that in His boundless love God knows what we need to live a life of perfect peace and happiness. That having been said, the remainder of this book will be focused on helping you begin your journey by finding ways to learn to trust God and, with that trust ways to find peace in your life—a peace that can only come from living within the love of God.

4

Debt Is Only a Symptom

*The covetous man is never satisfied with money, and the
lover of wealth reaps no fruit from it.*
ECCLESIASTES 5:9

Before we continue, I would like to address something
that may be an issue for you. While I have not kept it a
secret that my own religious tradition is that of Catholicism,
I am in no way stating or inferring that I believe that to
trust God one must be Catholic. The reality is that we hu-
mans created religions and denominations within religions,
and history has recorded far too many atrocities that have
been perpetrated against mankind for the sake of religion.

I believe that God is willing to use any religion to help
us be in a loving relationship with Him and is certainly
not limited to any one religion to do so. Yes, it is true that
I believe that the universe and all that is in it and of it
was created by God. As a Christian, I believe that, to heal

our broken relationship with Him, God chose to become human as Jesus, to live among us as one of us to show us how to live in relationship with God. To make it possible for us to regain the relationship we lost when we turned from God, He died and rose again. And I also believe that, to help us live in a loving relationship with God and His creation, God's divine spirit is infinitely present.

However, I want to be clear that I also believe that in His very act of creation, God loves each and every human being as His children with a love that far exceeds that of any parent and that He is simply calling each of us to an intimate relationship with Him. In all my biblical studies while working toward my Masters degree in Theology, I never found a single passage stating "thou shalt go to church." I don't for one moment believe that the extent of God's love for us is determined by or limited to the hours spent inside a church, or the number of committees we belong to or even the money we give to the poor.

In my simple way of thinking I have come to believe that, after thousands of years watching us continually mess up and stray farther and farther from Him, God decided to live on earth Himself to not only *tell* us, but to *show* us what He meant when He calls us to a loving relationship with Him. God's love is all-inclusive. He wants everyone to be in a loving relationship with Him in whatever way works for us. While I have chosen Catholicism as my community of people to support me in my journey with my heavenly Father, I believe the Holy Spirit will not be limited by our human delineation of religions and denominations.

I am not trying to recruit you or persuade you in any

way to choose a specific religion. I am, however, trying to share with you things that I have found to be true not only for me, but for all those who have come to understand the same truths. Believing whether or not what Jesus taught about God is true is a lot like whether or not you believe in gravity. You can't see gravity either, but even if you adamantly deny that gravity exists when you step off a ten-story building, you'll hit the pavement below with just as much deadly force as you would had you believed in gravity. And so I ask you to be like Isaac Newton. Open your mind to the possibility of God and His selfless love for you and perhaps, with the help of God, He will give me the words that will help you begin to trust Him in your life.

Are You Really Ready to Get Started?

Looking back at my own situation, I can see clearly that the actual blessing in my life was that I was truly desperate to change things. I wasn't trying to grow closer to God or find peace in my life. The simple fact was that I was miserable because every morning I awoke feeling a sense of failure. I had completely messed up my marriage because I screwed up our finances, and I didn't see a way to salvage either.

On the day I asked John to help me, in my mind I was saying, *I'll do anything to fix this—anything,* even if that means admitting that there may be something to this stuff my Bible thumping friend believes. Whatever . . . as long as it works, I'm in. And in my heart I was feeling, *God help me please. I'm really, really scared. I don't want to lose my family, and I think you're the only one who can help me.*

The blessing I speak of was that our financial mess

was something tangible I could deal with, something that I could focus on. Because of my sense of hopelessness, I was ready to place myself into the Hands of God. I knew I had caused my own problems. I knew that I had no one else to blame. On that awful yet wonderful night that I read Luke 12:22-34 for the first time, I was a broken man who just wanted to run to his Daddy to be held and reassured that things would be okay.

The first scripture verse that I memorized, Romans 8:28, was something John told me when I called him the next day which says: "All things work for good for those who love God, who are called according to His purpose." While I don't for one second believe that God causes bad things to happen, I have come to understand the meaning of this verse is, in His Divine love and mercy, God can use every situation to help us learn to live in a loving and trusting relationship with Him. And so, for me, the road that led me to the incredible adventure of a life centered on God was learning to handle money. So, too, perhaps, it may be for you. So how do you begin?

I think an important first step is deciding you will make a change. While that may seem like a simple and straight forward statement, it has been my observation that having the strength of conviction to stand by your decision makes the difference between success and failure. So I guess in some way it comes down to answering one question—how important is it to you to get your finances under control?

Perhaps a simple test for yourself would be to answer this question: as I suggested earlier, have you gotten out your Bible and read the books of Haggai and Malachi yet? Certainly, there are lots of reasons why you might not have done so: you don't own a Bible, you want to finish the whole book first to decide whether or not what I have to say is worthwhile, you think I made my point clear enough when reading the excerpts I provided, you aren't Christian and believe that the Bible is not for you. Regardless of the reason, if you haven't done so yet it is, perhaps, an indicator that you at least are not quite where I was. You see, once I decided to let go of my pride and trust God, I made a conscious decision to put my trust into action. That action manifested itself in seeking God's guidance wherever I could find it.

Since I believe that God was using John to help me find my way, I looked to John as my guide and mentor. So when he suggested I read a book, I purchased that book and read it within a matter of a few days. When John pointed me to specific chapters or verses in the Bible, I read them and re-read them many times. I found myself hungry for knowledge and was amazed at how much had been written about dealing with money from a biblical perspective as well as living a life centered on God. So when I would read a book and the author mentioned another book, I would get that book and read it next.

Perhaps you are thinking that it is impractical to think about reading as much as I did. I'm sure you are busy. Well, so was I. Because I was determined to change my financial situation, I knew that it was not enough for me to cut back on my spending; I needed to make more money. And so during this time I was doing what I needed to keep my

Navy obligations, while doing my forensic consulting work sometimes as much as fifty hours in a week and, on top of that, I was working a part-time business. But I have found that, when something is a priority, you will find time to do it.

So allow me to be as blunt with you as John was with me. If you are not satisfied with your current financial situation, what are you doing differently this year from last year to change your situation? Benjamin Franklin once said, "The definition of insanity is doing the same thing over and over again and expecting different results." To achieve different results, you must do something different. If time is your excuse, I challenge you to look critically at how you spend your time. In spite of our disastrous situation, Leslee and I still managed to bowl in leagues two days a week. I was playing racquetball at least one day a week while Leslee had softball games one or two days a week. And, of course, we had our TV programs we never missed! So is the issue that you don't have time or is the truth that you aren't willing to make the time? The bottom line is change is sometimes painful, and it certainly takes work.

While what happened to Leslee and me at times seemed almost miraculous, it is important that you understand that we worked our butts off and practiced delayed gratification with a level of patience I did not think possible. Trusting God gave us the belief that the work we were doing would pay off. In the beginning of this process, I never thought in my wildest dreams that I would be completely debt-free. I was just hoping that we could get out from under our credit card load and, after years of hard work, could get our debt down to only our mortgage. But as I said in the beginning, trust is something that is learned. And once I began to see that I really could trust God, I removed all limitations to what I thought we could accomplish.

So are you ready to get started on a new and awesome adventure? Are you ready to make changes in your life? Are you ready to let go and let God? Are you ready to live a life that most people only dream about? A life in which you have neither debt nor worries about money? A life where you are content with who you are and where you live? A life filled with love for your spouse and your children? A life where you can focus on ways to share what you have with others to make their lives easier? A life where you are aware of God's love in all that you do? A life of joy and peace?

While your journey may take different shapes and forms than mine or others I describe in these pages, I promise you that a life lived in a loving and trusting relationship with God is an amazing adventure. I also promise that, if you follow the principles I will share in the following pages, you will see amazing results. Not because you are who you are or because I am anything special, but because God is who He is, and He wants you to be happy and free from worry.

Debt Is Only a Symptom of the Actual Problem

We're just about ready to begin digging into the mechanics of eliminating debt in Part 2, but there is one more important concept for you to understand if there is any hope for you to achieve long-term success. Before a doctor can properly treat a patient, she must observe the symptoms and conduct tests to arrive at a diagnosis of the problem. The treatment, then, is prescribed to solve the problem which, in turn, eliminates the symptom. In that light, we must look beyond the symptom, which is debt, and diagnose the illness so that we can effectively cure the patient.

Let us begin by talking specifically about money and place it in perspective. While money plays a prominent role in one's day to day life, money, in its simplest form, is merely a commodity we give to another in exchange for something we need or desire. Currency in and of itself, whether in the form of paper or coins, has very little real value or use. Over time, society has placed value on silver and gold, which are somewhat rare natural ores, and the paper and coins we use to exchange for goods and services are based on the value society places on those ores.

During times of inflation, we become painfully aware of the seemingly arbitrary nature of that value. Yet because it is the means for exchange, people in all walks of life have become dependent on money. And because of the perceived importance of money throughout the ages, mankind has tended to measure a person's success or failure in life based on his/her ability to accumulate this vehicle of exchange. Far too often one's "importance" on this earth is measured by his or her financial status. As I shared with you earlier, I saw myself as a complete failure and almost destroyed my relationship with the woman I have loved for over thirty years simply because of our lack of money.

The reality is that we place far too much importance on money so much that it has been the reason for countries to go to war, lives taken, marriages dissolved, and friendships destroyed. I have often heard a verse from scripture misquoted stating "money is the root of all evil." The context of this quote is usually associated with the inference that money itself is bad and therefore, those who have lots of it are, in turn, bad people. Since money is simply an instrument of barter, it can neither be good nor evil so what's up with this verse? Let's begin by examining the actual verses from First Timothy.

> 9 *Those who want to be rich are falling into temptation and into a trap and into many foolish and harmful desires, which plunge them into ruin and destruction.* 10 *For the **love of money** is the root of all evils, and some people in their desire for it have strayed from the faith and have pierced themselves with many pains.* {1 Tim 6:9-10}

Thus, the caution to the reader of scripture is about placing too much importance on money, which can lead to ruin. It is not saying that there is something bad about money itself. However, I caution you to not take this passage too lightly. When first reading these words I initially dismissed them, thinking that they did not apply to me because, not only was I not rich, I didn't want to be. I seemed to have developed a snobbish mindset, perhaps from my Catholic upbringing, that rich people were selfish and greedy and were rich only because they did not care about others. I felt that I, on the other hand, lived a modest, middle-class lifestyle and cared about the plight of those less fortunate than I.

The truth was, however, that every waking moment of my life was driven by money. My poor decisions to buy things I couldn't afford had driven me to a position that I was truly controlled by money. As for my concern for the poor, I hadn't given a dime nor done anything else to help anyone in need for several years! I was too busy with my own problems to worry about others. Because of my debt, I had obligated myself to many, many people, and the pressure I felt about these obligations often made me quite uncharitable in my words to those I loved.

With this as a preamble, then, I suggest that the first step toward living in a loving relationship with God (which will include financial stability) is to take a page from the teachings of Buddha. On his path to enlightenment, Prince Siddhartha, who ultimately became the Buddha, observed that the key to inner peace was found in what he called the "middle way." After years of living an extreme ascetic life, Siddhartha noticed a passing boat on which was a teacher and his student. The teacher was explaining to the young student about tuning a stringed instrument, stating that if the string is too loose, it will not play, but if you tighten it too much, it will break.

From that simple statement Siddhartha reached an epiphany about his own life. As a young prince, he had lived a life of opulence in which he had not experienced any pain nor suffering, and as an ascetic, he lived a life of constant deprivation. In neither case did he experience a sense of peace or contentment. Thus, the foundation of the Buddhist way of life is *balance*.

Examine your life today, asking yourself if someone else were to scrutinize the way you live based on the hours you work, the time you spend with your spouse, your children, your friends, the house your live in, the cars you drive, the vacations you take and the luxuries you own, would she say you understand the principal of moderation? If you are like most, you work far too many hours, most likely to finance the lifestyle you've chosen to live. It's even possible that you are working a job or are in a field that you don't even like simply because it pays you the most, which in turn allows you to live the lifestyle you've chosen. While it wasn't a conscious decision that started you down this path, somewhere along the way you felt yourself trapped with the sense that there is nothing you can do except to keep chasing the buck to keep your head above water.

And how did you get here? By choosing to live beyond your means. Whether we are ready to admit it or not, each of us chooses the lifestyle by which we live. For Leslee and me, our choice almost destroyed our marriage. We were trying to live like those we knew and admired. We bought into the marketing propaganda by convincing ourselves that we deserved more. I vividly remember speaking with friends, explaining that we were young and our greatest earning potential was in front of us, so now was the time to be in debt because we had years to pay it off. The saddest part about it was that our friends agreed with us!

Balance begins by internalizing for yourself the principle of *moderation*. I'm not asking you to follow the example of St. Francis of Assisi by living a life of complete poverty. I'm simply challenging you to at least live within your means. At this point it is important to point out that the irrefutable formula for staying out of debt is to *spend less than you make.* As obvious as that may seem, it is a principle certainly not followed by our state or federal governments or the majority of households in America. Until you are ready to do this, it is not possible to get out of debt.

Therefore, it is my sincerest hope that you've made the decision to make permanent changes that will lead you to a debt-free life—one filled with the peace and joy that comes from walking confidently with God. The mindset needed for getting out of debt is similar to that of losing weight. It takes two important decisions. First, you must decide to lose weight by exercising regularly, eating less, and eating sensibly. But that is not enough.

Since I turned thirty, I have struggled keeping my weight down. I have found that each time I get fed up with myself and decide to drop weight, I am quite disciplined in the process and mechanics for doing so. The challenge I face is not losing it, it is keeping the weight off. There are so many good reasons for me to keep my weight down that have nothing to do with vanity. I know I have more energy, I sleep better, I am more flexible, and my endurance is much better. Additionally, my cholesterol is down, and my heart is under much less stress. In short, with the weight off I feel much better and significantly increase the probability of a longer, more healthy life.

Yet each time I lose weight, I still struggle to keep it off. Why? Because along with the decision to lose weight must come the decision to change the bad habits that cause the weight gain. The simple fact is I like to eat, and my weight gain comes from eating too much. It doesn't take a PhD in nutrition to understand that if you ingest more calories than you burn, you will gain weight.

So too it is with personal finances. If you spend more money than you make, you will accumulate debt. Thus, along with your decision to get out of debt *must* come the decision to change the spending habits that caused the debt in the first place.

PART 2

Assuming Control of Your Finances

The Church teaches that, when one goes out to do missionary work, the first step is to tend to the immediate needs of the people to whom you are reaching out. If they are hungry, you should feed them. If they are naked, give them clothes. And for those who are sick, care for their illness. By meeting their needs, the people will see Jesus in you, and no preaching is necessary. Besides, when you are starving, you are far too distracted by your hunger to hear anyone preach about the love of God.

So it is with this in mind that I have chosen to dedicate Part 2 of this book to dealing with what is worrying most people — financial matters. My goal is to help you eliminate the distractions caused by financial unrest, and it is my sincerest hope that, while doing so, you will discover an amazing relationship with God as your Heavenly Father.

You will notice a change in the writing style in this section as we move from storytelling to specific teaching of a financial process. I suggest you take a break before continuing. When you are ready to resume, sit at a table or desk with a hi-lighter, a pencil, and some lined paper. To reduce the size of the book, I have limited the extent of my examples, but have not left you hanging. When you are ready to begin to actually execute the process I describe, go to my website where you will find expanded examples, blank forms, and templates that you may download and use to set up the suggested ledgers. There are also links to other helpful sites. While on my site, note that there is a section in which you will find other practical suggestions for ways to manage your finances on a day-to-day basis.

www.patrickabrady.com

5

Getting Out of Debt

Owe nothing to anyone, except to love one another.
ROMANS 13:8

While there are lots of fad diets which say theirs is the best or fastest or easiest way to lose weight, the reality is that it takes discipline and hard work to effectively lose weight. So it is with getting out of debt. I assure you that the process that I am about to describe will not fail; the only variable in the method is the length of time it will take to achieve your goal. Recall in my story I said that my friend, John, warned me that, without addressing the spiritual component, his advice might not work.

To that end, when I began using the methods he showed me without trusting God for His help, I made little progress. I had little success increasing my income and, at the same time, seemed to be spinning my wheels in my efforts to pay off my debt. As I reduced certain bills, something would come up, such as a fender bender or a major appliance breaking down, that required me to charge the repairs and erase whatever progress I had made. After nine months of diligent effort to reduce my debt, we were, at best, at the same level of debt as when we began. It has been my observation that, when the individual includes tithing and fully trusts God for His help, the stumbling blocks seem to diminish if not vanish. That having been said, let's begin.

The actual debt elimination process that I am about to explain in detail is simple enough to be described in just a few sentences. First, figure out where you are spending your money, and if you are spending more money than you make (which is always the case or you wouldn't be in debt), take steps to stop doing so.

Second, cut your spending enough that you have money left over every month and use a portion of that additional money to pay down your debt.

Third, calculate the total of your monthly debt payments and add it to the portion of the left over monthly income that you have chosen to use for debt elimination. Then commit to applying that entire amount towards your debt every month until you have no debt remaining.

Fourth, beginning with the creditor with the lowest balance, make the required monthly payment and add to it the additional money you chose to use to eliminate your debt and continue applying the extra money toward that one debt until it is paid off.

Finally, once the debt with the lowest is retired, begin working on the next lowest balance by applying all the extra money to it until it is eliminated. Because the total amount you are spending each month remains the same, each time you move to the next lowest balance, the amount you are applying to that creditor will be larger than the amount paid towards the previous creditor, thereby reducing the number of months it will take to pay it off.

I said the process is simple, but it is not necessarily easy.

Where Are You Spending Your Money?

When I work with couples to help them get control of their finances and get out of debt, they come to me assuming I will begin the process by talking to them about a budget. However, most people don't know how to set up or live within a budget. Without question, the foundation for sound financial stability, whether we're speaking about the federal government, a major company, a small business or a family, is a balanced budget. Put simply, a budget is a detailed estimate of how much money an individual or entity will earn on an annual basis compared to the estimated expenses that will be incurred during that same year. A budget is said to be *balanced* when the total of the income and expenses are equal. In a situation where there is more estimated income than expenses, the excess income is referred to as a *surplus*, and when there is not enough income, the excess expense is called a *deficit*.

Clearly, my goal is to help you get to a point where your annual budget shows a surplus. However, creating a budget is not where I want you to begin. While the key to effectively managing your finances will be living by a budget, what you need to do first is to get a clear picture of where you are spending your money. So for the next two months, I want you to account for *every* dollar you spend. This process of tracking all the money you spend is called a *cash-flow analysis.*

Much of the money you spend on a monthly basis is easy to track because it takes the form of a monthly bill such as your mortgage, utility bills, phone bills etc. for which you write a check or pay electronically. However, the area of spending that typically gets people in trouble is when they spend cash or charge something on a credit card. Therefore, the main focus on this two-month cash-flow analysis will be keeping track of those types of expenditures. Don't be surprised if in this process you find you cannot actually account for every dollar you spend in the first month.

To help you with the cash component of your analysis, I suggest that you keep receipts for everything you purchase, even if it is only a dollar or two. Place two boxes on your dresser and, at the end of every day, put the cash receipts for the day in one box and your credit receipts in the other. At the beginning of each day, write on a piece of paper that you will leave in your cash box, the exact amount of cash you put in your pocket/wallet/purse and leave that paper in the cash box. At the end of the day subtract the cash you still have from the amount written on the paper. The difference should be reflected in your receipts. If the total of the receipts falls short, do your best to write on the paper what you purchased without a receipt, and if you are still short, add a line item called *unaccounted,* next to which you write the amount.

To track your spending, create a spreadsheet or ledger, and at least once a week record the purchases reflected in your boxes, separating cash from credit. When you receive your monthly statement for your credit card(s), you should check the statement against your receipts, in case you made charges for which you did not keep the receipt.

Since, in financial management, knowledge is power, I suggest that you invest in an inexpensive software package that will enable you to easily track your spending on a continuing basis. While there are several programs on the market, I have found that Quicken is a user friendly and inexpensive program that is intuitive in nature and easy to start up. Should you choose to purchase this program, I suggest you do it right away so that you can use it during this cash-flow analysis phase. If you are not quite ready to begin using some type of software program, you can go to my website and download some simple spreadsheets and blank forms that will assist you in tracking your money.

NOTE

Don't get intimidated by terms like ledger or spreadsheet, for as you can see in my example, this can be something as simple as a hand-written piece of paper. While this process may seem cumbersome and time-consuming, I assure you it is necessary and helpful. If you will commit to following this procedure daily, I think you'll find that your unaccounted number will continue to diminish as the days pass. I also have a blank form on my website which you can use for tracking your spending.

While the main purpose of this analysis is to help you establish a baseline for a budget, a nice side benefit is that it becomes quite eye-opening in identifying wasteful spending habits. I vividly remember one young couple who, at their first session with me, came to my house each carrying a Super Big Gulp which they had purchased at 7-11 on the way to our meeting. After completing their cash flow analysis, they came to our next session and explained

how astonished they were by the many ways they frittered
their money away. To their surprise and embarrassment,
they found they had been spending over $75 a month on
Super Big Gulps alone! Then, with a sheepish smile, they
asked for a glass of water. For many, just the knowledge
of where their money is going becomes the first step to
cutting back.

Stopping the Bleeding

With your income and expense ledgers complete, you
should be able to see whether or not your net income is
greater than, equal to, or less than your outgo. Most important is that you will have a very detailed accounting of the
makeup of the outgo. As was the case for Leslee and I and
many others, your outgo may exceed your income, which
is referred to as *negative* cash-flow. If you do have negative
cash flow and your objective is to get out of debt, then it
is essential for you to find ways to reduce your spending
as quickly as you can to at least *neutralize* your cash flow
(income = outgo).

So now it is crunch time. Do you really want to get out
of debt? I have found that often most people will quickly
answer yes to this question yet many of them find it difficult to actually begin the work necessary to attack their
debt. There always seems to be something that prevents
them from pulling the trigger.

Years ago, I was in the hospital because I was having a bad episode with my back and hips related to my
shipboard injury. The pain was so intense that I couldn't
walk for about a week. I was in a VA hospital, and the

doctors were baffled by the severe onset of the pain and even more confused at the sudden and complete cessation of the symptoms.

On the fourth or fifth day in the hospital, I was being examined by yet another doctor to whom I complained rather rudely how disappointed I was in the VA hospital. In exasperation, I told her that she was the fourth doctor I had seen in as many days and, after repeating the same explanation of symptoms and watching her look at the same test results, like the doctors before her, I had to listen to yet another medical professional explain that she had no idea what was wrong.

After patiently listening to the whining of this grumpy patient, this woman looked me in the eyes and said, "While, like the others, I am unsure of the reason for the abrupt starting and stopping of the pain, I'm quite certain that if I was as fat as you are, my back would be killing me! Quite frankly, Mr. Brady, you need to lose at least seventy-five pounds right away. Your body is telling you that you are excessively overweight."

After a few moments of trying to collect myself from such a blunt statement, I responded by trying to explain to her that while I knew I was overweight, the pain in my back and hips prevented me from exercising enough to keep from gaining weight. And then, as I gained more weight, the more pain I experienced, which in turn made me less physically active. Without flinching she smiled at me and said, "Mr. Brady, that is a crock. Regardless of your excuses, the simple fact is you are too fat." Each time she called me fat, I cringed inside. "So I suggest that your first step should be to stop eating so much."

After trying to offer more excuses, it became clear that she wasn't about to accept them. She finished by telling me that, since my symptoms were gone, there was no reason for me to remain in the hospital any longer. She told me to go home and lose weight, and if I was still in pain after I had lost at least seventy-five pounds, to come back to see her and she would be happy to examine me to explore the medical causes of my pain.

So I went home and got serious about losing weight. How I did it is not important. The bottom line was I stopped making excuses, changed my eating habits, and figured out ways to exercise. In the beginning the exercising was painful, but as I began to lose weight I found that I could exercise more with less pain. And in nine months I lost eighty pounds, and because I felt so good, I found no need to return to the doctor. Since then, each time I slip back into my bad habits, I gain weight, and when I do, the pain returns. Because the pain manifests itself most significantly in my hips, you could say that for me being overweight is truly a pain in the butt!

The point of this story is that, regardless of what your reasons or excuses for over-spending are, if you want to get out of debt, you must do something about it. There is a term in many self-help books that if taken to heart, would dramatically decrease the prevalence of personal debt in our society. That term is "delayed gratification," which simply means to have the discipline to put off short-term pleasures today for a greater reward in the future. Athletes describe it by saying, "No pain, no gain." Just as I was told to stop eating so much, your first step is to stop spending so much.

The difficulty we all face is that delayed gratification goes completely against what we hear and see in the media. Throughout the day, whether over the radio, on television, or on billboards, we are bombarded with the message to buy now and pay later. What most people do not realize is that chasing after the toys, gadgets, and trinkets with money they don't have today is keeping them from an awesome life of peace and security tomorrow. The fact is that before 1950, outside purchasing a home, unless they had the cash to pay for something, people just didn't buy it. Practicing delayed gratification is an essential component to your long-term financial stability.

So once again I say it's time to go to work, even if it means doing things you don't want to do. If you have negative cash flow, you must stop the bleeding. And with the same bluntness my doctor used to address my weight problem, I say to you, if you have negative cash-flow and you like to go out to dinner three to four nights a week, stop—you can't afford to. If you have negative cash-flow, you need to immediately examine both your social life as well as your standard of living.

Begin examining your purchases with the question of whether or not what you are purchasing is something you *need* or something you simply *want*. Do you really need two new pairs of shoes? What's wrong with those you have? Do you really need a big screen TV? What's wrong with the one you have? Is the new computer you want going to help you do your job better or will it just make the non-productive games you play or web browsing faster? This type of questioning can and should be applied to every aspect of your spending. But are you in enough pain to begin developing the discipline to say to yourself, "No, not now." Delayed gratification doesn't mean you'll never be able to purchase nice things or do the fun stuff; it means having the discipline and character to tell yourself that you can wait until you have the cash to pay for those things you simply want.

For Leslee and me, our work began with examining our cash flow ledger to see what we could immediately cut out. Part of our challenge was we really didn't go out to dinner much or own expensive or trendy clothes. We had never done any traveling that wasn't associated with a moving van and didn't participate in what many would call the night scene. Our debt problems developed because our mortgage and car payments alone consumed about 60% of our monthly income. However, we did go to the movies two or three times a month, which included the cost of a baby sitter. Additionally, we were both in two bowling leagues, which also involved a baby sitter the nights we bowled together. I also belonged to a fitness club, for which we made monthly payments.

Knowing how far we were in debt, we didn't hesitate to drop all these activities immediately. In fact, we felt that, as we were taking an honest look at everything, it seemed almost irresponsible for us to continue spending money in that way. What are some things you can think of that you can eliminate to reduce your monthly spending?

The difficulty we faced was, even after cutting out all the *extras* and creating a budget as cost effectively as we could, our outgo was still greater than our income. We didn't have enough income to pay all our bills even if we made only minimum payments on our credit cards. If we didn't charge anything more, our choice was to skip a payment of a few credit cards or continue relying on Leslee's parents to feed us several nights a week. The good news is that it has been my experience when helping couples with their debt reduction, that to stop the trend of negative cash flow, most people simply have to re-evaluate how they spend their money on recreation and entertainment and what some might call recreational shopping.

Because of his background as a CPA, I asked my son to review this section and point out any areas that needed clarification or fine tuning. In regard to making adjustments in your spending to develop a positive cash flow, Matt said that from the many taxes returns he files he believes that, for most people, developing a positive cash flow is a simple matter of deciding to do so.

The cash-flow analysis will quickly identify the areas of unnecessary spending and then it is up to the individual make a decision to reverse the pattern. He points out that, while there will be some who will have trapped themselves from making poor decisions as Leslee and I did when buying a house, most are simply spending money on more discretionary items or activities than they can afford. However, if that alone does not fix the problem, more significant steps can and must be taken.

Knowing that we had to turn our cash flow to at least neutral (getting our outgo to match our income) our next step was to look at what we owned that we could sell to pay off some of our debt and eliminate payments. So we had several garage sales at which we sold furniture, clothing, bowling equipment, racquetball rackets, record collections etc. Using the local paper to advertise, we were able to sell bigger ticket items such as our piano and larger more expensive power tools that I had begun to accumulate.

To help improve our cash-flow, we traded in our Honda Civic, which we had purchased new and for which we were making large monthly payments, and bought a used four-door economy car that was perfectly functional and netted us a monthly payment about half of what we had been paying with a much lower principal balance. We also sold our second car, which was a Mazda pickup that we purchased new, and with the little money we made from the sale of the truck plus the proceeds from selling our piano, were able to pay cash for a 1971, mustard yellow and rust Datsun pickup truck that looked awful, but ran like a champ.

From the outside looking in, it may have seemed like the Bradys were moving backwards financially. But the truth was these two kids who had been married for six years were beginning to grow up and accept responsibility for their lives. What was changing was our attitude regarding what other people thought of us and our recognition of what was really important to us. We may not have been keeping up appearances, but we were definitely making headway.

The most significant sacrifice by far came from my wife. One evening Leslee came to me and explained that she had taken her engagement ring to be appraised and found a jeweler who was willing to buy it for 75% of the appraised value. Without the least hesitation, Leslee insisted we sell her ring. Looking back, I see now that this gesture became a turning point for me. This selfless act was Leslee's way of showing me that she understood we were in this together and was willing to do whatever it took to make things work.

Her conviction gave me such strength. That evening in my alone time with God I thanked Him for giving me the gift of such an amazing wife, a woman who chose to love me and not condemn me for my shortcomings. In my prayer, I promised God that once He had helped us get out of debt and stabilized ourselves enough to have a little extra spending money, the first purchase I would make would be to replace Leslee's ring.

Perhaps as you read about the things we did you may wonder if you will be willing to do the kind of things Leslee and I did to get out of debt. You may be thinking that you're not that desperate or maybe that you don't want to get out of debt that badly. Maybe you're thinking, what if I do all this stuff and it doesn't work? In fact, when discussing some of the things I was writing about with my brother-in-law, he asked an earnest question of me. "What happens if someone who reads the book does everything you say to do and they go broke anyway?" My response is simple; trust God.

The process I describe for organizing your finances and systematically paying off your debt is not something I've devised. It is a proven method used and taught by many financial professionals which I successfully applied to my own circumstances. What I bring to the discussion is the spiritual dimension, which includes the principal of tithing. And I tell you without hesitation, if you do as I am suggesting—truly trust God—He will not let you fail. Leslee and I are not religious fanatics who are blindly willing to drink poison cool aid. We were two reasonable adults who had seen God's hand move in amazing ways in our life.

We were willing to sacrifice the things we did because we were confident that God was working with us and that all we sacrificed was for something much better later. In fact, my answer to this question highlights the focus of this entire book. Because of what I've experienced, I have absolutely no doubt about the existence of God and the love He has for me. Not only do I know God loves me as only a perfect father can, I know that, as long as I am willing to trust Him and include Him in all I do, I can live every day with peace and confidence. As King David said,

> ^{1} *The Lord is my shepherd; there is nothing I lack.* ^{2} *In green pastures you let me graze; to safe waters you lead me;* ^{3} *you restore my strength. You guide me along the right path for the sake of your name.* ^{4} ***Even when***

I walk through a dark valley, I fear no harm, for you are at my side; your rod and staff give me courage. [5] *You set a table before me as my enemies watch; you anoint my head with oil; my cup overflows.* [6] *Only goodness and love will pursue me all the days of my life; I will dwell in the house of the Lord for years to come. {Psalm 23}*

A little over three years after we sold Leslee's ring, when we had paid off all our debt except our mortgage, I took Leslee to that same jeweler and watched with such pleasure as she ordered a Naval Academy miniature for which she was much more excited than the original engagement ring. Once again, my partner for life spoke volumes to me. For in wearing a miniature of my class ring, Leslee was showing others that she was proud to be married to me.

Creating a Budget

Having tracked where you are spending your money and taken the necessary steps to neutralize your cash-flow, you will be ready to create your initial budget. Remember that a budget is a tool to help you plan where you intend to spend your money in order to maintain a positive cash-flow position. For the budget to be effective, you should continue tracking your spending and record it monthly, so that you can compare your actual spending to your budget to see how you are doing. *(I address the practice of using a budget in a short video on my website.)*

Take two pieces of paper and on the top of one write "Monthly Income" and on the other write "Monthly Expenses." Beginning with the Monthly Income sheet, list down the left side each separate source of income you have. To the right of each item write the amount you take home each month. For any income items that are not monthly, take the annual amount, after taxes, divide it by twelve and write the monthly amount next to that item. Finally, at the bottom of the page calculate your total monthly net income.

Similarly, on the Monthly Expenses sheet, I would like you to list everything you've been tracking for the past two months. Try to simplify where possible by placing certain items in categories to reduce the actual length of the list. There will be items that are not actually monthly in nature such as insurance premiums and some utility bills for which you will need to calculate a monthly amount.

You will begin to see in tracking your daily spending, there are many things for which you've been paying cash that vary in nature. For any item that occurs less frequently than monthly you'll need to estimate an average monthly amount, and for those cash items you'll also need to make your best estimate as to how much you will typically spend each month. (If this average is high, it should be the first thing you look at to reduce your spending.) It is useful to list the items in reverse order of magnitude. For example it is likely your mortgage payment or rent is the largest monthly expense, then your car payment. At the end of the list, calculate the total monthly spending which we will call outgo. If your total income is greater than your total outgo, the surplus is considered *discretionary* income, a portion of which can be used for reducing your debt.

So let's review what we've discussed so far. First, you must take a couple months to track your spending so you can carefully analyze your buying habits. Second, if you have negative cash flow, you must take *whatever steps are necessary* to at least neutralize your cash flow. Third, you develop a working budget based on your needs (not wants) and current debt that will give you a positive cash flow (however small that may be).

NOTE

To help in this step I have put a blank form in my website called "Budget Work Sheet" that you can print and use to write the information you are collecting. Once you are ready, you can also download an Excel spreadsheet and use it to track your actual monthly expenditures. On my site, I also go into more detail regarding income withholdings and ways to maximize your monthly cash-flow.

Let the Healing Begin

Okay, now that you've stopped the bleeding, it's time to work on the actual healing process. When examining your cash flow, there are two sides to your ledger — income and outgo. To eliminate your debt, you want to take action on both sides of the ledger. The attitude Leslee and I had was that we were young and full of energy and could always sleep when we were dead, but for now it's time to work. Because we had eliminated recreational things like bowling and racquetball we realized we could find ways to use that time to earn extra money. While circumstances will be different for each person working on his/her debt, we were prepared to take on one or two part-time jobs each to increase the income side of our ledger. As I shared with you earlier, this is where God really stepped in for us. Doors of opportunities to earn more money seemed to fly open for us

Because it is such a crucial aspect of my message to you, I want to be sure you understand that, from the very beginning of this process, we gave 10% of our gross income away to various charities. When explaining this, I am frequently asked about the specifics in my tithing practice. Therefore, I will devote some time later to explain ways that I use that have worked well for me.

Attacking the Debt Side of the Ledger

At this point in the process you will have managed to get your spending under control and, by cutting back, perhaps selling unnecessary items, and increasing your income, you will also have achieved a positive cash flow, meaning there is money left over at the end of each month. The next question to be answered is how to most effectively use that extra money to begin attacking your debt.

With your income and expense sheets out, take another piece of paper and write on the top of it, "Personal Debt Summary." This sheet is going to help you organize those monthly expense items for which you are making monthly payments. On this sheet I want you to list all your debts from biggest to smallest down the left side of the page. Next to each debt write the current balance, interest rate, and monthly payment. In the case of credit card debt, write the approximate minimum monthly payment. Table 1, to which I will refer in explaining this process, is a hypothetical example of how it should look. Note that the last item on the ledger reflects the sum total of your debt as well as the total monthly payments for servicing that debt.

Next, take the Monthly Expenses sheet you created earlier and draw a line through each item that is repeated on your personal debt summary sheet. What should remain should be items like insurance premium payments, telephone and utility bills, groceries etc. You are now ready to create your working "Budget Ledger." This ledger represents how you intend to spend your money each month, working diligently to not spend any more than what you've budgeted.

NOTE

To help you keep the end goal in mind, I want to point out that once you have completely eliminated your debt, the items remaining on your Monthly Expense ledger will be the only expenses left on your budget! How sweet will life be then? What will you do with all that additional money?

Personal Debt Summary

Creditor	Current Balance	Interest Rate	Monthly Payment
Home Mortgage	$300,000	6.00%	$2,248
College Loan	$26,000	3.50%	$150
Her Car Loan	$24,000	5.00%	$453
His Car Loan	$12,000	4.50%	$223
Furniture Co. Loan	$5,600	10.60%	$180
VISA CC #1	$5,400	12.50%	$63
Department Store CC	$2,800	13.10%	$47
Build Mtrl Store CC	$3,300	12.50%	$43
Master Card CC #1	$2,600	11.60%	$45
Master Card CC #2	$1,250	11.80%	$28
VISA CC #2	$1,300	13.20%	$35
Total Debt	$384,250		
Total Debt Service			$3,515

Table 1

The first line at the top of the ledger should be called "Total Net Income," and next to it write the number from your Monthly Income ledger. Following this line will be a list of all your expenses. I suggest that the first item listed is your tithe and the second item is labeled "Total Debt Payment," which you will take for your Personal Debt Summary.

Then list by reverse order of magnitude the other monthly expense items from your original expense page that have not been lined out. Table 2, to which I will also refer while explaining this process, is a hypothetical example of how the Budget Ledger should look. The last item on the Budget Ledger reflects the total of your estimated monthly outgo. With a positive cash-flow, the monthly total on this page should be less than your total net income. Using my two examples, you will see that the total monthly outgo including payment towards your debt is $6,990 and, based on the income in my example in Table 2, you have $510 additional money at the end of the month.

Does this seem boring or tedious? I hope not. I hope you will feel a growing sense of excitement as you begin to understand your financial situation. Remember, knowledge is power! This knowledge will give you the power to change your financial situation and thereby your life. Plus, by the time your reach this step you will have made significant progress.

Having reached a point where you have positive cash-flow, I would suggest you take between 50-75% of the additional money you have each month and commit that money to debt reduction. For this example I will use 70%

Budget Ledger

Total Net Income	$7,500
Tithe	$750
Total Debt Payment	$3,515
His Car Gas/Oil/Repair	$200
His Car Insurance	$75
Her Car Gas/Oil/repair	$200
Her Car Insurance	$75
TV/Internet/Phone (Bundle)	$150
Both Cell Phones	$100
Life Insurance	$150
Home Repair/Maintenance	$100
Utilities: Electricity/Gas/Water	$250
Groceries	$650
Kids (diapers, shoes, sports fees)	$175
Medical (prescriptions, copays, etc.)	$100
Entertainment (dinner, movies, bars, etc.)	$500
Monthly Outgo	$6,990
Left Over Cash	$510
75% for Debt	$383

Table 2

of the excess money, which will be $357. Therefore, as we begin the debt elimination process in this example, you would commit to applying a minimum of $3,872 ($3,515 + $357) to service your debt. While as your income increases you are encouraged to add to that number, I ask you to firmly commit to applying a minimum of $3,872 to your debt until it is *completely* eliminated.

NOTE

It is at this point in the process when things get exciting. It is far easier to explain this concept by speaking with someone while drawing on a board or flip chart. Therefore, I recommend that if you find yourself getting bogged down in reading this explanation, you go to my website to view a few video clips where I personally explain this process. Don't get so caught up in trying to follow the precise numbers that you lose sight of the overall concept.

Accelerating Your Payments

It's not enough to commit to spending a fixed amount to debt reduction. Knowing where to apply that money makes a huge difference. The most effective way to eliminate your debt is to learn how to *accelerate* your payments one at a time. By developing the Debt Summary Table (Table 1) you have a tool to help you make payment decisions.

Basically, you are looking to pay off the account with the smallest balance first and then work your way up to the largest balance, systematically increasing your payments with the additional money available as you pay off creditors.

Looking at my example in Table 1, note that you have two items, MasterCard CC #2 and VISA CC #2, that have similar balances with similar interest rates, but VISA CC #2 has a higher monthly payment. Because it has a higher monthly payment, which consumes more of your cash flow, you'll want to pay that debt off first. If the payments were similar, you would want to attack the one with the higher interest rate first.

Starting at the bottom of your debt summary, first apply the additional $357 to the $35 payment for VISA CC #2. By paying $392 a month towards VISA CC #2, you will be able to pay it off in full in month four.

Since in the fourth month the balance on VISA CC #2 will be $124, apply the remaining $268 towards Master Card CC #2 ($268 + $28 = $296). By applying the $28 monthly payment over the past three months, plus the additional $296, the balance at the end of month four on Master Card CC #2 is $870. Therefore, with the *accelerated* payment of $420 ($357 + $35 + 28) you will pay off Master Card CC #2 in three more months, leaving $390 remaining in the third month to apply to Master Card CC #1. With two credit cards eliminated your accelerated payment will now increase to $465 ($357 + $35 + $28 + $45). Continue applying this new amount until you have eliminated Master Card CC #1.

From this point forward, you simply repeat the process over and over again, watching the size of your accelerated payment grow larger and larger and the number of actual payments diminishing along with their remaining balances.

IMPORTANT...IMPORTANT...IMPORTANT

To help you with your decision to also stay out of debt, I STRONGLY urge you to include a note with your final payment to VISA CC #2 company requesting them to CLOSE your account. If you are married I also urge you to take a moment with your spouse and say a prayer of thanks to God asking Him to continue guiding you in your quest. Then if you have a shredder drop that sucker in the machine and celebrate as it grinds it to bits!

Stay Focused and Don't Let Up

There are two key components to this method. The first is having the discipline to commit to applying the total amount of debt service to your budget even after you begin to pay off creditors. It can be quite tempting to ease up and reward yourself for making progress. Don't do it. There are ways to reward yourself that cost little or no money. Regardless of how you choose to celebrate, be sure that the money you spend on your reward is money available after you have paid your entire monthly debt service. The second key component is to apply as much additional money to debt service as you can, as the opportunity presents itself. Leslee and I were able to completely pay off our credit card debt in six months following this method, by applying every possible dollar we could towards our debt.

The financial blessings we began to see during this time in our life were astonishing. In our case, it seemed like the more money we gave away to those in need, the more money we made. But in spite of all the money we were making, Leslee and I remained committed to keeping our expenses down. We chose not to go out to dinner or the movies and we only went to social events with friends or family when it required minimal expense.

To some, this may seem extreme or too great a sacrifice, but we saw it as a way of showing God we were committed to working with Him to get out of debt. Our goal was to be 100% debt free and paying off our credit card debt was simply a step along the way. In place of bowling, racquetball, the movies etc., we found ways to spend time together at home with our kids. Our volatile relationship, that had been filled with tension and anxiety, gave way to wonderful intimate evenings where our love and romance was rekindled. Looking back, these were awesome times. Our simple prayer was for God to help us fix our marriage. Who would have guessed that His answer would come from the two of us working hard together and sacrificing for each other to get out of debt?

Just eighteen months after beginning this process,

we had eliminated a significant portion of our debt. What remained was our mortgage, one car payment, and one last consolidation loan. It is usually at this point that people begin to get skeptical. Some suspect that I may be exaggerating the time frame or think that the only way I was able to achieve such a short time table was because I was making huge amounts of money to overcome our situation. So before we continue further, let us examine the time table of the hypothetical example I've just described. (On my website, I have built a financial model that will back up the following statement.)

By adding an additional $357 to the $3,515 you were already paying each month on your debt, using the accelerated payment method as I described, and taking interest into account, it will take approximately thirty-five months to pay off everything on Table #1 with the exception of the two car payments, the student loan and the mortgage. In fifty-six months the only debt remaining would be the mortgage and an additional $20,000 net income each year to apply to your mortgage principal!

So if that can be accomplished with just $357 extra a month, how much shorter would this timing be if the additional payment was another $200 higher than that? Thus, the reason my personal timeline was so short was because, for the first year and a half, we not only paid the fixed amount we committed to, we also applied every spare dollar we received to our debt. I believe that, like us and others who have followed this method, once you begin to see how quickly it really can happen, your determination to keep the ball rolling will increase as will your willingness to apply extra money when you have it.

In January, 1985, I was out of the Navy and selfemployed, earning a very good income. With a mortgage, one car payment and a consolidation loan we were still applying accelerated payments towards our debt, but had also begun an aggressive savings program. After assessing our situation at that point, we made a very important decision. Our oldest son, Matthew, was in first grade and his younger sister, Kathleen, was beginning pre-school and Leslee felt it very important for her to be a full time mom again. While the income she made was nice, it certainly was no longer essential. As I encourage you to do, we continued to apply the minimum debt service payment, which by then had been increased significantly from where we began. However, we chose to reduce our level of discretionary income and the amount we were saving in order to allow Leslee the ability to quit her full-time job and begin to fully live her vocation as a mother—and what a wonderful mother she has been.

Shortly after quitting her job, by the grace of God, Leslee had a third baby whom we named, Maureen. Because of our improved financial situation and Leslee's choice, our children have no memories of a mother who worked outside our home. When our oldest daughter, Kathleen, began high school, Leslee chose to pursue her passion for sports by coaching varsity field hockey and girls' lacrosse at the high school our children attended. For the past twelve years, this amazing woman has taken her love for God, children and sports and built an amazing varsity program that has positively touched the lives of hundreds of teenage girls. By placing God in the center of our life, Leslee has had the freedom to pursue what she was called to do and not work at a job that she was compelled to do by a life lived chasing worldly pleasure.

In short, stay focused, trust God, and be willing to do whatever it takes to get out of debt. The reward is a life of peace and true freedom to do whatever you feel called to do.

6

Live Within Your Means

Do not conform yourself to this age but be transformed
by the renewal of your mind, that you may discern what
is the will of God, what is good and pleasing and perfect.
ROMANS 12:2

 B efore I continue, this would be a good time to check back in with you, the reader, regarding the Christian perspective and reasoning that guided me in my journey. I stated earlier that I am quite confident that what I have experienced in eliminating my debt and building a confident relationship with God is intended for everyone regardless of their personal religious beliefs. While I am not trying to proselytize, I find it impossible to explain the truths I've learned on my journey without sharing with you how I've come to understand many of these discoveries.

Moving forward, I will continue to use passages from the New Testament that have played significant roles in my understanding of life. While the latest census statistics show that two-thirds of the population of the world do not acknowledge the Christian belief in the divinity of Jesus, I feel comfortable in saying that most people will agree that Jesus was a remarkable figure whose writings about love and forgiveness have profoundly impacted the world. Just as the writings of Buddha, Confucius, Aristotle, Muhammad, Gandhi and Martin Luther King, Jr. are renowned for the wisdom they impart, when I speak of Jesus perhaps you can also consider the wisdom in His words.

For the most part I have been writing with the assumption that, like me, you are, or were, severely in debt and are struggling to make ends meet. Yet there are some who may be reading this book who are not living in dire straits, but are living on the outer edge of their earning potential. Perhaps you own a beautiful home, drive nice cars, belong to a country club, dine frequently at nice restaurants, and vacation at least once a year at very resorts. And you do this without worrying about paying your bills.

To you, I pose a few questions. Does your lifestyle require both spouses to work full-time? If so, and you have young children, would Momma prefer to stay home to care for them? What percentage of your monthly income does it take to make your mortgage payment? Are you planning on paying off your home in less than thirty years? Are you making payments on your automobiles? Are you paying your credit cards off in full each month? How much money are you saving each month? How much money are you giving away? Most important of all, how much would your lifestyle change if you or your spouse are laid off and/or took a 30% pay cut? In short, are you living above, within or below your means?

Regardless of your initial circumstances, the net result of controlling your spending and paying down your debt is ever increasing discretionary income. It may seem almost inconceivable at the moment that you could ever be free from the frustration and angst associated with living paycheck to paycheck, but I assure you, if you will trust God and include Him in your daily efforts, the time will come (I believe sooner than later) that your questions will shift from "where is the money going to come from" to "how can I best use the money I have?"

A fundamental principle I taught my children when they were young is, if you can't handle money responsibly when you have just a little, don't expect to be able to do so when you have a lot. Therefore, you need to prepare for the time when you do have more money than expenses by learning to manage what you have now. First and foremost, regardless of the size of your income, I encourage you to recognize that whatever income you receive is truly a gift given freely from God. The questions that only you can answer are: 1) How will you use this gift to adequately care for you and your family today and in years to come? 2) How will you share some of this gift with those less fortunate than you?

I believe that a key component to living within your means depends on how you define *adequate*. We are all familiar with the expression "beauty is in the eye of the beholder." The same holds true for judging adequacy. To a homeless man living on the streets of Baltimore in winter, a warm room with a bed and blanket would be heaven. Yet to an eighteen-year-old, who grew up in a well-to-do family, living in a college dorm and eating the food in the school dining hall, without the use of Dad's credit card may feel unacceptable. The question that Jesus consistently presented to those who wanted to follow him was, how much is enough?

To the rich man who asked what he needed to do to have eternal life, Jesus responded "Go, sell all you have, give it to the poor, and follow me." But this was not meant as a directive to us all. Scripture scholars point out that Jesus knew that for the man in the story, his wealth was preventing him from living life as God intended—one who is concerned with the needs of others rather than with the accumulation of personal wealth. The danger in wealth that Jesus warned about comes when things we own become a higher priority than our love for God and our neighbor. The most important lesson I have learned in my fifty-six years on this earth is that, like the Apostles, we must be *willing* to drop everything, leave all we know and love, to follow where Jesus leads.

And so I suggest that living within our means requires a change of heart. Some might even say it is a surrender of our will to God's love. We must continually answer for ourselves the question Jesus poses, how much is enough? Such a question is so pivotal in nature that I believe every married couple needs to carefully discuss and explore how they will answer it as a family. Together, they need to define for themselves the difference between *wants* and *needs* and agree on priorities. I find that the identification of priorities will naturally determine the lifestyle one chooses. However, it is important to recognize that the priorities in our lives change over time along with changing circumstances. Thus, this is an ongoing conversation within a family. It is, indeed, a challenge in every relationship to consider both the needs as well as the wants of our partner.

How much is enough? As you begin to eliminate your debt and have more discretionary income, this is a question I hope you and your spouse ask each other often. Just because you have the cash to purchase something does not necessarily mean you should. When I was learning to distinguish between wants and needs for myself and my family, I decided to use the life of Jesus to be my guide. Jesus was a man who, based on my Christian belief, was also God, and as God, Jesus voluntarily chose to accept human limitations. If you were Jesus and had the ability to do *anything* you wanted, how tempted would you be to take the easy path?

Certainly, He could have dined on the finest food available to man. Certainly, He could have displayed his power and proven his divinity and been the most powerful man on earth. Most significantly, He could have avoided the torturous death He endured by allowing His angels to come to His aid. Yet, out of love for us, He chose to demonstrate how to live a truly loving and fulfilling life. Jesus lived a totally selfless life. His daily actions were others-centered and never self-centered.

The Buddhists teach a similar message when telling the life of Siddhartha before he became the Buddha. As the heir to the throne, Prince Siddhartha could have anything, but he chose a life that was others-centered. He chose to dedicate his life to teaching others to look beyond themselves. In his struggles to break the cruelty and oppression of the Arab nation, Muhammad spoke frequently of the importance of caring for those in need. He, too, could have had the opportunity to have whatever material wealth he wanted, but chose, instead, to live for others.

I am not suggesting that we all shave our heads and wear a toga like Gandhi, nor that we sell all we have and join a monastery. I am suggesting that when answering the question of how much is enough, we consider the needs of others in our decision.

When considering this question for ourselves, Leslee and I began to understand that we are all susceptible to peer pressure (whether directly or indirectly) through carefully produced marketing tools. As our children were growing up, we constantly monitored the kids our children hung around with, knowing how influential others can be. Why is it that we think that influence stops once we've grown up? As I began to examine my life, I could see so many ways that I was letting society, and more specifically, those around me influence the decisions I made.

There was a certain level of stature I wanted to maintain. After all, I was the president of a big company making the big bucks. Of course, I should be driving a late model luxury car and living in a big home. I bought Leslee a Rolex watch and lots of expensive jewelry because that's what a woman of her position should have. It didn't matter that Leslee is much more comfortable in gym shorts and a T shirt, with a whistle around her neck and a clip board in her hand. Coaches don't need a Rolex, they need a digital watch with a stop watch feature. How can you grip a golf club or field hockey stick with diamond rings all over your fingers? The fact was, Leslee not only didn't need that stuff; she really didn't even want it. But I bought them for her anyway because that is what I thought was expected of me.

I suggest we take a page from Buddha's teaching by living a life of balance. Just because you can afford to buy something doesn't mean you should buy it. Our current national crisis is based on rampant consumerism. For too many, shopping has become a form of recreation, so much that when you listen to the economic experts speak during downturns in our economy, they base their forecasts for the rate of recovery on how willing Americans are to purchase without concern. When the unemployment rate is high, people are less likely to spend money at the rate they would when unemployment is low and the economy is good. The irony of a consumer-based economy is that the more people are saving money and not spending it on frivolous things, the longer it takes to recover in times of a recession. Now that's out of whack!

Allow me to suggest some things to consider that may help you begin to achieve some financial balance in your life by examining areas that most would consider necessary items in their lives.

Choice of Home

Buy vs. Rent: While the American dream is to own your own home, whether you should buy or rent is certainly a legitimate question. Because of the equity component of ownership and the tax advantages associated with mortgage interest, purchasing a home is an attractive option. I believe that the decision should be based on four factors.

The first factor, cash flow, is simply a math issue. Assuming you are making an apples to apples comparison of places to live, if the monthly cash outlay for purchasing a house is equal to that of renting, then by all means, purchase. When making this comparison, you should also take into account the reduction in cash outlay that comes from the mortgage tax break. After getting the advice of a qualified tax professional, you may find that even if your total mortgage payment may exceed what you would pay in rent by 10-12%, you are still better off purchasing versus renting.

Location: The second factor to consider is location. First, do you feel safe in the area? If Mr. is away on business, will Mrs. feel safe at home alone? Will you feel safe walking with your kids or letting them play at the neighborhood park? How far is this home from work? Long commutes can certainly test one's patience and add pressure to a marriage relationship. Will the development in which the house in located likely appreciate in value?

Size: Probably the most important factor to consider when purchasing a house is size. If it is your first home, consider whether or not the size will meet your needs for at least five years. Before purchasing a home, I challenge you to evaluate what your needs are regarding a home. It's easy to let emotions lead you in this area. Is the home you're considering what you need or is it what you want? Are you thinking about how it will impress your family and friends? Is it a matter of pride that you buy versus rent? Do you think owning a single family home versus an attached townhouse will give you more status? Do you really *need* three bedrooms and a two-car garage?

Over the past twenty years I have watched the size of new homes increase significantly. As a kid, I grew up in a 1,500 square foot, four-bedroom home with a family of eight children and I don't ever remember complaining about being cramped. In the suburbs of DC and Maryland, it is not unusual to see young couples today purchasing 4,000 square foot houses as a *starter* home. So please be conscious of the lures of modern marketing.

Material Condition: Finally, after carefully considering what is an adequate size to fill your needs, you should consider material condition. While most homes will require some minor repairs and cosmetic improvements, I strongly discourage first home buyers from purchasing a *project*. First and foremost, you should be purchasing a house to be your home. I believe that purchasing a house that is to be your primary residence simply because it is a good investment is a mistake.

A good example would be a newlywed couple who feels they are pretty good at do-it-yourself projects deciding to buy a *fixer-upper* for their first home. Their reasoning is that they can get a house under market value and, because they are a little handy, plan to do lots of improvements themselves. It has been my observation that while in theory, this may be a way to make a good profit when they sell the house, it is a potential train wreck waiting to happen. The first couple years of marriage are tough enough without adding the complication of living in a construction zone and spending all your *free* time working on the house. Without the balance of spending quality time together working on their relationship, this young couple may find themselves splitting whatever profits they make on the sale of their house in their divorce settlement.

When choosing a house, carefully consider how much time and money will be involved in transforming this new house into your home.

Cars: Status Symbol or Transportation

Unless you live in a large urban area with ample public transportation, a car, for most people, is considered a necessity. The question to be considered is what kind of car? Contrary to media hype, a car is not an investment, yet more and more people are financing car purchases for as long as ten years as if it were an investment. Cars are expensive enough as it is. How much more are you willing to pay for a car because you financed it? With few exceptions, cars begin depreciating in value immediately until they are eventually worthless.

While you may not be able to pay cash for your next car today, just like there is a proven method for getting out of debt, there is also a proven method for reaching a point where you can pay cash for every car you purchase for the rest of your life. The initial cars you drive may not be the type that will wow your friends; however, I promise that if you're patient and disciplined, the quality of cars will improve.

Step number one is to live by the adage, *If you can't pay*

cash for the car, you can't afford it. Okay, so you don't have the money to buy any car, period; what now? The simple answer is to finance your purchase, but with a cautionary caveat. The car you finance should be the least expensive car possible. To do this will require that you check your ego at the door when shopping for a car. To most Americans, a car is a status symbol that makes a statement about who we are.

I suggest that, rather than worrying about *who* others think you are, that you remember *whose* you are—a uniquely loved child of God who wants for you a life of peace and joy. If you are already saddled with car payments on a new car, I suggest you explore avenues to sell or trade that car and down-grade to a car that will provide adequate transportation with the lowest payment and principle balance as possible. Then, following the debt reduction plan I showed you earlier, pay the car off as soon as you can.

To reach the point where you can pay cash for a car, the concept is quite simple. Once your car or cars are paid off, you continue to drive them as long as the maintenance costs make sense. While still driving the car you now own outright, begin making car payments to yourself in a separate savings account. We'll discuss the amount of the payment a little later. Let's say you are able to go another eighteen months before it's time to replace your car. You now have whatever trade-in value that remains on the car as well as the money you've been putting aside each month for the past eighteen months. Perhaps this is still not enough money to purchase a car outright. The trade-in and the saved money will certainly make a good down payment on the car, which will allow you to finance much less this time.

Ideally, this next car should be an inexpensive used car about three years old with no more than 20,000 miles on the odometer. Even if you could do it for less, I suggest you finance the car for three to five years to minimize the monthly payment. Hopefully the payment will be much less than the payment you've been making to yourself for the past eighteen months. Thus, each month you make that same payment on the loan that you were making to yourself, you will be applying much more to the principle and, therefore, pay the loan off in a shorter period of time. As soon as you satisfy the loan, you resume making payments to yourself and, because you've purchased a late model car in good condition, you should easily get 5 years with this car.

Now, five years down the road, you're ready for a new car and, because you've been making payments to yourself, you have a pretty good chunk of change saved in your "car payment" account. If you shop wisely, you should be ready to purchase your first car with cash. From this point forward you continue to make your monthly car payment to yourself and, if you like, there is no reason you can't replace your car every three to four years. If you want to begin to upgrade the type of car you drive, then simply increase your monthly payment, and if you take good care of your cars, you should still have some decent trade-in value at the three year point.

As one who has purchased over twenty cars in my lifetime, I would like to share with you the lessons I've learned about that process. Regardless of your income level, I believe it is foolish to purchase a car new. It is common knowledge that any automobile, regardless of make or model, will depreciate at least 10% as soon as you drive it off the lot, and as much as 40% within the first three years. So why not let someone else pay for that depreciation? Because there are lots of people who, for a number of reasons, only hold on to cars for one to two years, there are some great buys for practically new cars with low mileage on them.

As an example, the car I currently drive, which I bought in the spring of 2009, is a Mazda Miata. It is such a fun car that it actually replaced the 2001 Miata I was driving before it. The new car is a 2006 model, had a little less than 12,000 miles on it, was still under warranty and looked brand new. In fact, unless I said something, no one would have known it was used. The only difference is that I paid about 60% of the sticker price of a new Miata. When comparing it to the 2009 model, the differences are insignificant and almost imperceptible. While this may seem like no brainer, it took us purchasing four new cars before we saw the light!

Making Payments to Yourself

Determining the size of car payment you make to yourself is simply a function of your cash flow. Estimate the time frame during which you'll need to purchase your next car, guess at the price, and divide it by the number of months. If your cash flow will allow it, make that payment. If not, make as large a payment as you feel comfortable. In regard to putting the money aside, I found that I needed to be a little creative to help discipline myself in this area.

While it is not so much the case these days, twenty years ago I found that I needed to hide money from myself to keep from being tempted to spend it. Whether it is the money I was putting aside for permanent savings, for a car or for the kids' college education, I found I needed to put it somewhere that I was not routinely reminded I had it. So I would pick financial institutions that were not directly connected to the bank that contained my regular checking account. There are lots of options in the banking industry that should allow you to deposit money into a money market type account where you can maximize interest as the balance grows.

The key for me was it had to be an account that I did not routinely see or think about and took extra effort from which to withdraw funds. Also, to reduce the temptation, I set up direct deposits with my employer so that the savings payments were automatically taken from my paycheck and placed in the various savings accounts.

Discretionary Income

When referring to discretionary income, I am speaking about income available after meeting all of your financial obligations. Thus, it is income that you spend at your own discretion. This becomes an important talking point before wrapping up this chapter because the use of discretionary income can be a source of much tension in a family relationship. This friction usually is a result of a differing opinion on wants versus needs and personal priorities. I will not presume to offer an opinion on what should or should not be a priority for you. However, I would like to offer a few suggestions that might help you work with your partner in dealing with discretionary income.

Let's start with the most basic form of discretionary income, which is what many will call spending money, or pocket money. While this may be one of the smaller line items on your budget, I have found that it is a frequent source of high volume discussions between married couples. Leslee and I have experimented with many different ways to handle this area until we found a method that has been working well for us for almost ten years. Allow me to explain.

Because in our home we have chosen for Leslee to be a stay-at-home Mom, I have been the primary income producer for the Brady family for most of our married life. The difficulty this presents to Leslee is the sense that the money I earn is my money and not really hers and, therefore, she feels like she must take extra care when spending money and, at times, feels she needs permission to buy things. Leslee has shared with me that no matter how much I may say it is *our* money, she *feels* like it is my money and not ours.

Over the years, we have had many discussions (some at high volume, some involving tears) around this topic, and I have admitted to Leslee that in some instances she is correct in that I do think of it as my money. However, regardless of how either of us feel, the reality is we are one family and we needed to find a way that both of us can comfortably spend the family income. For most, this is not difficult to do when it involves the necessities such as mortgage, food, or things for the kids. The area that triggers the friction is when we wander into the realm of personal discretionary spending. Let me describe what we did to deal with this.

Our first step was to discuss what things that individually we may purchase with cash or credit cards that we both considered to be necessary items for the family. These were things like lunch money or field trip money for the kids, gas for the car, groceries, school supplies, and dry cleaning. Things that we considered to be personal would be eating out instead of eating at home, anything recreational such as going to the movies or playing golf or purchasing new clothes just because we thought they were nice. It doesn't matter what the actual items will be for you; the important thing is to agree on the items. Once we decided on what things were necessary in the course of our days, we then agreed that anything else would be paid for with our *spending* money.

Next, we decided that each of us would carry a different credit card, which we would use to purchase the necessities. We chose to use separate cards as a way to keep each other accountable for our spending. Finally, we decided on a fixed amount of cash we would draw each week to use as our personal spending money with the understanding that our spouse could not question or critique our use of this money. The deal is that, if we run out of cash before the end of the week, we have to wait until the next week for our next draw. So the trick is to manage the cash to last the week.

Over time, both of us found that there were weeks we didn't spend all the money, and independently we chose to use the accumulated money to purchase something extra special (often for each other). As a matter of practice, each week when we take our next draw, I take any money I have left from the week before and put it in a drawer because, even today, I know that the more money I have in my pocket, the more I tend to spend.

Especially when you are in the initial stages of debt reduction, I strongly recommend that you adopt this type of strategy. When initially getting control of your spending, you should be conscious of how you are using ATM machines. If necessary, you should break the habit of running to an ATM each time you are running low on cash. Besides the unnecessary costs involved with out of network fees, ATM hopping can easily lead to unplanned spending. Every Thursday I go either to my branch bank ATM or one that is in network and does not have a local fee to draw our weekly spending money. We chose Thursday because we tend to spend most of our money on the weekends so that allows us to load up at the beginning of the weekend.

The second area of discretionary spending I want to address is purchases that are $500 or more. Because, by its very nature, discretionary income can be used on anything you like, the controlling factor for such a purchase should be the parameters agreed upon by both spouses. Of course, if you are single, you may not have someone to challenge your sanity. In our case, Leslee and I have agreed that neither of us will make a purchase greater than $500 without discussing it with the other first. Whether it is something as small as new golf clubs or a new computer or as expensive as a boat or vacation property, it is important to communicate with one another to understand each other's priorities.

Because we had to tighten our belts so much in the early years of our marriage, Leslee and I have made vacation travel a priority for us. In our later years we try to take two to three nice trips a year. Because of that, we have made what I believe were pretty expensive mistakes in purchasing vacation properties. Without going into the painful details, let me share with you some costly wisdom. When the time is right, I encourage you to travel and make memories with your loved ones. But in doing so, save your money and pay for your vacation one trip at a time. Do not be fooled into paying for vacations you *might* take some day.

In general, when dealing with discretionary purchases, avoid impulse buying; take a few days to think about any purchase over $500 before signing anything and, men, listen to your wives!

Assessing Your Priorities

In wrapping up this discussion on living within one's means, we must address the root cause of either the success or failure of any person or family to live comfortably within their financial resources. I submit that virtually every time we spend money, that decision to spend should be made based on our priorities in life. The tricky part is that too often, we're making fiduciary decisions without consciously recognizing or acknowledging our priorities.

Earlier, I spoke of the importance of husbands and wives discussing each other's priorities. This should be a fluid discussion, one revisited time and again since life is always in a constant state of change. Some years ago, Leslee and I attended a weekend couples' retreat which centered on assessing our priorities. Throughout the weekend, we listened to various married couples speak about meaningful ways they have used to engage in such discussions, and methods to deal with differences in order to reach a consensus.

The most fruitful part of the weekend for us was listening to the keynote speaker present the concept of *vertical alignment*. The premise of this principal is that when we align our priorities with God, we are working within His natural laws. Just as it is much easier to swim with the current than against it, aligning ourselves with God makes the journey much more pleasant. That weekend, we were taught to live in sync with God's priorities where our vertical alignment of priorities should be:

God

Spouse

Children

Career

Using this alignment as our compass, we have been able to identify the times when we were drifting off course, and found it easier to identify the corrective action to help us regain our direction. I wish I could say that since that powerful weekend we have always been in agreement with our priorities and have lived a blissful, balanced life, but that would be a lie. However, like any good compass, it has been a very effective tool for us to navigate through our difficult times.

How Are You Navigating on Your Journey Through Life?

Using the vertical alignment I just described, would you say that you are in sync with God and with your spouse? Because one's relationship with God is so personal let me simply ask you to honestly consider where God fits in your consciousness on a daily basis. You, alone, are the only one qualified to make that assessment.

The second priority level, however, is often outwardly visible. The question to be answered is do you put the needs of your children ahead of your spouse? A wise person once pointed out to me that our children are with us for just a few short years, but our vow is to be with our spouse for the rest of our lives. Because there are so many ways that we can get this out of balance, I urge you to be on guard and frequently reflect on how attentive you are to your spouse. Kids have a knack for demanding our attention. However, our spouse can be dangerously silent.

Please don't interpret this to mean that your children should be left to fend for themselves. In fact, some might argue that if your calling is to be a father or mother, then one of your highest priorities is indeed to devote sufficient time and attention to their upbringing. But how much better will you be able to raise your children if you and your spouse are already on the same page and have made meaningful efforts to care and love one another? By making your spouse a priority, you are indeed making your children a priority. One of the greatest gifts parents can give their children is to make sure their kids grow up seeing how much Mom and Dad love each other.

Finally, let me address your career. Especially when placed in the context of finances, getting out of balance with one's career is an enticing trap. I often hear someone admit to being a *workaholic*. While it is intended to have a negative connotation, this statement is frequently stated with a hint of pride, like wearing a badge of honor. As one who has fallen into this trap, I sincerely hope you will take heed to my warning.

With the clarity of hindsight, I will tell you that to nurture and grow a healthy, loving relationship, a family must spend time together. While it doesn't have to be 24/7, it most certainly must be more than a few hours a week. I recognize that there are times in our lives when circumstances demand that we get out of balance. However, when we do, we need to be conscious of its occurrence and work at regaining balance as soon as possible. And until we do regain balance we should seek ways to compensate for the imbalance.

For example, when we were preparing to take FTI through its initial public offering (IPO) I realized that during that phase it was going to be necessary for me to travel extensively. Even when in town, I knew that I would be working late hours. In anticipation of this intense time, Leslee and I called a family meeting during which we told the kids what was going on at Papa's work. We felt they were old enough to understand, so we explained what an

IPO was and why it was so important not only for the company but for us as a family. Then we asked the kids if there were some things happening in their lives that they wanted to be sure I was home to watch or be involved in.

After each child was given the opportunity to prioritize his or her list of things for Papa, I promised to work my schedule around each of their top two to three items. I then explained to the CEO that those commitments were in stone. Before we ended our family meeting we made plans with the kids to do a few fun family events that gave us all something to look forward to during the grind.

When discussing professional careers a very sensitive area is whether or not both spouses should work outside the home. While I personally would like to see one of the parents at home in every family, I recognize there are those who would disagree with me. There are certainly individuals who are much more fulfilled having a business career, yet also love their children and are wonderful parents. Suffice it to say that when making the decision of whether or not mom or dad stay home to care for the kids there are many factors that come into play. Thus, when making this decision, I urge you to use the vertical alignment model to assist in weighing the pros and cons.

Listening to a talk radio station, I heard a discussion about how much maternity leave the average mother takes before returning to work. The radio host was interviewing an expert in this area who was offering tips on ways the new mom can "stay plugged in to work" while she's still at home with junior. This was then followed by ways to survive the six or so weeks when mom is on unpaid maternity leave. The last hurtle discussed was finding good day care for the child.

As I listened to this discussion, it occurred to me that not once did the conversation venture toward a discussion of either mom or dad staying home to care for their children. The implication in the interview was that the norm is for both parents to work outside the home. Yet there are many households in which, given the opportunity, mom would gladly stay home to care for her children. When discussing this section with my daughter, Kat, she told me that most of her friends who are working moms tell her how much they would love to stay at home but they just can't afford to.

In the case of a family where both parents are working simply because it is financially necessary, then I suggest, when executing your debt elimination plan that you begin to seriously explore ways to reduce your cost of living sufficiently enough to be sustained with one income.

With your vertical alignment as your guide, you could consider changing the home you live in and the cars you drive. Is it better for your children to go to private school with both parents working than going public to school so mom or dad can be there when they get home from school? Maybe it will mean a second job for the spouse who continues to work outside the home or finding a way for the stay-at-home spouse to earn money while still caring for the kids?

The choices are not easy, but if it is your priority for one of the parents to be home, then I believe that with God's help, there will be a way.

For each of our children, it was important that, when the babies started coming, mom stayed home. To make that a reality, I encouraged my kids to base their lifestyle on one income. During the initial years of marriage it is fine for both spouses to work. In fact, it is a great way to get ahead in the savings department, as long as you never make any financial decisions involving long term commitments that require both incomes. Then, when the babies come and mom stays home, you won't miss her income.

I assure you it can be done. Even in the high cost of living area of DC/Baltimore, my children are living proof. Both my daughter-in-law, Melanie, and my daughter Kat have been home with their children since their first child was born. Likewise, my daughter Maureen and her husband, Tom, have been living off one income since they got married.

To summarize this entire chapter let's keep things simple. Living within your means is all about managing priorities. If discussing priorities is a routine practice while using the vertical alignment of God, spouse, children and career as your benchmark for assessment, any conversations you have about money should take place with little or no emotion.

7

Developing the Habit of Saving

*They should collect all the food of these good years that
are coming and store up the grain under the authority of
Pharaoh, to be kept in the cities for food. This food should
be held in reserve for the country, to be used during the
seven years of famine that will come upon Egypt, so that
the country may not be ruined by the famine.*
GENESIS 41:35-36

Until now, my focus has been on giving you practical
methods for getting out of debt and spending your money
wisely without speaking at all about saving. Saving money
is an important principle for financial security that over
the past twenty years in this country has seemed to have
become a lost art. Just doing some quick searches on the
Internet, it becomes obvious that while the numbers vary
from source to source, the United States consistently ranks
among the lowest savings per household of all the non-third
world countries. I found reports showing that over the past

ten years, the average savings per household fluctuating from a negative figure to never higher than 5.5%.

What that demonstrates is that the vast majority of Americans live above their means, e.g. spend more than they make and far too many have little to no money in savings. The day Leslee and I hit our knees asking God to help save our marriage, we had been married for seven years and had less than $100 in savings. Oh, how I wish we were the exception to the average American family, but I know there are far too many people in a similar situation.

Whether you are out of debt completely, have only a mortgage, or are working your way out of debt, this discussion on saving money applies to you. When I was battling to get my head above water, I chose to delay putting money in savings for the short term, using all my excess cash to reduce my debt. However, such a move should only be an emergency measure and not considered throughout the entire debt elimination period. Sticking with the concept of committing to a fixed amount of money until your entire debt is retired is a sound principle. However, as your income increases, it would be wise to begin putting some of your excess cash into savings.

To help you develop a healthy savings mentality, I strongly urge you to read a book by George Clason entitled *The Richest Man in Babylon*. It is a quick read written in the form of a parable that clearly describes a principle which I call "permanent" savings. Whenever I work with an individual or a couple to help them with their finances, I make reading this book a prerequisite before working with me, so perhaps you can make *The Richest Man in Babylon* your next read after this.

The essence of *Richest Man in Babylon* is understanding human nature in that we can live off 90% of our income just as easily as 100%. From a strictly secular perspective, Clason teaches that, before you do anything else with your money, pay yourself 10%—in other words, always save 10% of every dollar you earn. While I don't disagree with Clason, I must reiterate that everything we have is God's in the first place, so the first thing we do with the money which God has entrusted to us is give back to the needy in the name of God. Then we pay ourselves (save). However, unlike tithing, which I began doing immediately at the 10% level, I worked my way up to saving 10% during my debt elimination phase. But before I get too much farther ahead of myself, allow me to explain the principle behind *permanent* savings.

A financial planner will refer to the type of savings described in *The Richest Man in Babylon* as retirement savings. The reason I call it permanent savings is because I try to instill in each person the mindset that it is money that, once placed in savings, is never ever touched. In fact, many of the couples I have worked with prefer calling it "never-to-be-touched" savings.

Because this is such an important idea, I have chosen for the past five years, as I've taught religion to high school seniors, to take a couple class periods to explain this principle to my students. The table on page 118 is the same teaching tool I use with them and is a hypothetical example of what would happen if an individual began saving 10% of his or her gross income as soon as he/she entered the work force and continued to do so for the rest of his life. Because I teach college prep students, my assumption is that they will go to college and begin earning money at the age of 22. I will discuss the assumptions I made in developing this hypothetical model. Certainly the fluctuations in the market would be cause for challenging of some of my assumptions, but it is the theory I am trying to teach, so please don't be distracted by the details.

Because I want my students to begin developing the habit of saving, I tell them that throughout their four years in college, even though they will spend those years complaining about being "broke" college kids dreaming about the time when they get a real job and begin making real money, my model assumes that they save $300 a year, which is about six dollars a week. The initial salary is based on the typical demographic profile of my students who grew up and will likely live and work in the DC/Baltimore area. As an aside, based on the latest census bureau data for this area, my salary numbers are significantly below average. Note that at age 32 there is a significant jump in household income.

While I would like to see those who have children choose to have a stay-at-home mom or dad, I am assuming that most will be two income families. Also note that I am assuming that they get married at age 32. My next big jump is at 40. I chose this as a catch-up age because there are a multitude of financial surveys that state that we reach our peak earning potential between the ages of 40 and 50.

Therefore, I picked a number and froze it for the rest of the working life of the model. I would also like to point out that this assumption is in 2031, and in 2009 in the DC/ Baltimore metropolitan area that number would be low.

Having explained my assumptions, this is what I want you to get from the model. First, that you make the commitment to saving 10% of every dollar you receive, whether it is from a salary, a gift, a garage sale, or a lottery ticket. I'd like you to note in the model that at age forty (eighteen years after you enter the work force) you have set aside $115,700, but because compounding interest and long term market performance, your actual permanent savings balance is $105,829 higher.

It is at this point that I typically get one or two students raising their hands asking when they finally get to spend this money, to which I respond, "You don't." That usually gets a mixture of quizzical faces and frowns. I then point out to them and now to you, the bolded line at age fifty three. At that point you have set aside $310,700 but have now exceeded one million dollars in savings. Of course, the question returns, "Now do we get to spend it?" to which the answer is again "No." Once again, I point you to the next bolded row at age sixty at which point I am going to assume you will choose to retire. Note that your total contribution is $415,700 with a retirement balance of $2,078,009.

So now that you have retired, it is time to live off the *interest* from your retirement fund and, in my example, I have you drawing $100,000 per year, which is significantly less than the net gain each year. Therefore, by age seventy-five, the model shows a net gain of your account by an additional $2,000,000.

It is at this time that I point out to my kids that there is an important aspect of all this that must not be overlooked. If one does not live within his/her means, this model or anything similar is not possible. However, if you trust God, reject the guiles of society pointing to materialism, live a life of moderation, and are debt-free, you can live a life that is great—one that is financially secure and filled with a sense of peace and contentment.

What could you do with $100,000 a year if you have no debt? Can you see that retirement is not a function of age, that it is, in fact, driven by that last column in my model? And in my case the right column was such that I chose to leave the business world at the age of forty-eight with the promise to God that I would serve Him in any way He would lead. Little did I know that the path He would choose was to teach religion in a Catholic high school!

In my lifetime alone I have seen our economy go through record-breaking highs and scary lows. Because of the nature of a free enterprise-based economy, the market will continually experience corrections in both directions. Therefore, when developing a savings plan for your retirement and your family legacy, you must think long-term. When times are good, we must fight the urge to be greedy, and when they are bad, we must not panic. The message I want to leave with you is, regardless of the condition of the economy or the national administration in place, our individual financial future will always be our own responsibility. So start saving now!

Tips for Effective Saving

In response to my directive to save, the obvious question is where is the best place to put the savings? In no way do I claim to be an expert in the area of investing. In fact, the few times I attempted to invest on my own when I was younger, I lost money. When considering where to invest, I would like to give you a few things you might consider.

When the money you are investing is for *permanent* savings, keep your projected retirement age in mind. In general, the closer you are to retirement, the more conservative you should be. This should not be money to risk on speculative investing. If an investment opportunity looks too good to be true, it likely is. While you want to maximize the return on your investment, I don't think it's wise to try to look to the stock market as if it were a casino.

The vast majority of individuals that invest in the stock market attempting to pick one or two *good* stocks, lose money. That is why the large investment funds exist. The portfolios of these large market funds are successful because they are managed by experienced professionals who spread the invested funds across a large number of diverse stocks with the objective of more stocks performing well than those that are under-performing. By purchasing a significant number of different stocks, even if a few are doing very poorly, the downturn is diluted and thus, reducing the impact of the overall portfolio.

Since the money you are setting aside is intended for use ten to twenty years in the future, you should consider investing it in a financial product that can provide high yield long-term without pressure of short-term access. Thus, the first place to explore is some type of Individual Retirement Account (IRA) which will offer pre-tax benefits. Like putting money away for your next car, the most pain-free way of setting money aside for permanent savings is through payroll deduction. And because this is permanent, the best avenue would be through your company 401k plan. Most 401k plans give you options of where to put your money based on your personal risk tolerance. Thus, in making your decision within the 401k, keep in mind that the closer you are to retirement, the less risk you can afford to take.

There is one other important reason for using your company plan. Most companies have an employee benefit with some form of matching program for your 401k contribution. If you have such a program where you work, then take advantage of it. It is free money!

Beyond saving for retirement, there is also the need for short term savings. It is always good to put money aside for the proverbial *rainy day*. While the amount is mostly a function of your own risk tolerance, most financial advisors would recommend that you have at least three months salary in a savings account to which you have unrestricted access.

There are two savings practices that I have taught my kids that have been very effective for me. First, when receiving a pay increase, hide some of it before you ever see it. By that I mean, before you receive the first paycheck that will reflect your raise, make arrangements to have a portion of that raise deposited direction into a savings account. Since it was money you weren't used to seeing, you certainly will never miss it.

The second practice involves how you deal with the change in your pocket or purse. For many years, it has been my practice at the end of every day to take whatever change I have in my pocket and put it in a large container. Further, I make it my practice when making a cash purchase to always use bills and not reach for my change to come as close as I can to the total purchase price. In doing this, I have even more change in my pocket at the end of each day. This simple practice adds up to a significant number of time. In any given year, my personal *keep-the-change* program results in an annual savings between $400-$700.

As soon as you feel you've stabilized your financial situation, begin saving even if it's just your change. Then, once you are comfortable with your debt reduction plan, begin a consistent savings plan that is moving toward 10%.

Permanent Savings Model
Is It Worth Putting Aside 10%?

Year	Age	Annual Household Income	Annual Savings	Cumulative Savings	Savings w/ Compound Interest	Annual Interest
2009	18	-	$300	$300	$305	1.5%
2010	19	-	$300	$600	$609	
2011	20	-	$300	$900	$914	
2012	21	-	$300	$1,200	$1,218	
2013	22	$30,000	$3,000	$4,200	$4,345	3%
2014	23	$30,000	$3,000	$7,200	$7,565	
2015	24	$35,000	$3,500	$10,700	$11,397	
2016	25	$35,000	$3,500	$14,200	$15,344	
2017	26	$35,000	$3,500	$17,700	$19,409	
2018	27	$40,000	$4,000	$21,700	$24,814	6%

Year	Age	Annual Household Income	Annual Savings	Cumulative Savings	Savings w/ Compound Interest	Annual Interest
2019	28	$40,000	$4,000	$25,700	$30,542	
2020	29	$45,000	$4,500	$30,200	$37,145	
2021	30	$45,000	$4,500	$34,700	$44,144	
2022	31	$45,000	$4,500	$39,200	$51,562	
2023	32	$75,000	$7,500	$46,700	$63,787	8%
2024	33	$75,000	$7,500	$54,200	$76,990	
2025	34	$75,000	$7,500	$61,700	$91,249	
2026	35	$75,000	$7,500	$69,200	$106,649	
2027	36	$75,000	$7,500	$76,700	$123,281	
2028	37	$80,000	$8,000	$84,700	$143,097	9%
2029	38	$80,000	$8,000	$92,700	$164,695	
2030	39	$80,000	$8,000	$100,700	$188,238	

Year	Age	Annual Household Income	Annual Savings	Cumulative Savings	Savings w/ Compound Interest	Annual Interest
2031	40	$150,000	$15,000	$115,700	$221,529	
2032	41	$150,000	$15,000	$130,700	$257,817	
2033	42	$150,000	$15,000	$145,700	$297,371	
2034	43	$150,000	$15,000	$160,700	$340,484	
2035	44	$150,000	$15,000	$175,700	$387,477	
2036	45	$150,000	$15,000	$190,700	$438,700	
2037	46	$150,000	$15,000	$205,700	$494,533	
2038	47	$150,000	$15,000	$220,700	$555,391	
2039	48	$150,000	$15,000	$235,700	$621,727	
2040	49	$150,000	$15,000	$250,700	$694,032	
2041	50	$150,000	$15,000	$265,700	$772,845	
2042	51	$150,000	$15,000	$280,700	$858,751	

Year	Age	Annual Household Income	Annual Savings	Cumulative Savings	Savings w/ Compound Interest	Annual Interest
2043	52	$150,000	$15,000	$295,700	$952,389	
2044	53	$150,000	$15,000	$310,700	$1,054,454	
2045	54	$150,000	$15,000	$325,700	$1,165,704	
2046	55	$150,000	$15,000	$340,700	$1,286,968	
2047	56	$150,000	$15,000	$355,700	$1,419,145	
2048	57	$150,000	$15,000	$370,700	$1,563,218	
2049	58	$150,000	$15,000	$385,700	$1,720,258	
2050	59	$150,000	$15,000	$400,700	$1,891,431	
2051	60	$150,000	$15,000	$415,700	$2,078,009	
2052	61	$0	-$100,000	$315,700	$2,156,030	
2053	62	$0	-$100,000	$215,700	$2,241,073	
2054	63	$0	-$100,000	$115,700	$2,333,770	

Year	Age	Annual Household Income	Annual Savings	Cumulative Savings	Savings w/ Compound Interest	Annual Interest
2055	64	$0	-$100,000	$15,700	$2,434,809	
2056	65	$0	-$100,000	-$84,300	$2,544,942	
2057	66	$0	-$100,000	-$184,300	$2,664,986	
2058	67	$0	-$100,000	-$284,300	$2,795,835	
2059	68	$0	-$100,000	-$384,300	$2,938,460	
2060	69	$0	-$100,000	-$484,300	$3,093,922	
2061	70	$0	-$100,000	-$584,300	$3,263,375	
2062	71	$0	-$100,000	-$684,300	$3,448,078	
2063	72	$0	-$100,000	-$784,300	$3,649,406	
2064	73	$0	-$100,000	-$884,300	$3,868,852	
2065	74	$0	-$100,000	-$984,300	$4,108,049	
2066	75	$0	-$100,000	-$1,084,300	$4,368,773	

8

Stewardship

Without cost you have received; without cost you are to give.
MATTHEW 10:8

A popular term used by the church today is "Steward-ship," which is an Old Testament term. In the times of the people who are described in the book of Genesis and Exodus, there were individuals who filled the role of steward. In those times a steward was a servant who was tasked with managing all or some portion of the affairs of his wealthy master.

In Genesis we read of the interesting life of Joseph, the favorite son of Jacob, who was sold into slavery by his jealous brothers only to rise to the position of chief steward of the Pharaoh of Egypt. While Joseph was still a slave and owned nothing himself, as Chief Steward he was responsible for overseeing and managing everything in Egypt. Thus, he was the second most powerful man in the land. And because he took good care of everything the Pharaoh owned, Joseph was rewarded with an opulent lifestyle. Biblical scholars point out that it was because he always acknowledged his dependence on God that Joseph was able to rise from slavery to a position of great power.

I have come to understand that virtually everything we have in life is but a gift from God. Whether it is our life, our health, our spouse, our children, our talents, or our wealth, all are simply gifts from God. From His endless love, God has freely given us everything we have and He simply asks us to take good care of these gifts.

Like Joseph, each of us is a steward called to care for those parts of God's kingdom that He has entrusted to us personally. As good stewards we are called to care for what we've been given in a way that is pleasing to our master. And since Jesus taught us that the greatest two commandments are to love God above all else and to love our neighbors as ourselves, perhaps the best litmus test of how we are caring for our gifts is to ask ourselves in what way we are using our gifts to show God that we love Him and are caring for His creation.

I have had the opportunity to attend the International Catholic Stewardship Conference, an annual conference conducted in the United States and Canada at which clergy and lay people from around the globe gather to speak of ways to instill in the hearts of all Christians the principle of Stewardship. While stewardship certainly includes the principle of tithing, our income it is much broader in scope.

Stewardship takes into account our complete relationship with God, acknowledging that all we have and all we are is a gift from God—a gift freely given which He expects us to nurture and share freely. Thus, at the conference I was taught that we should view stewardship as a three-legged stool: time, talent, and treasure. God calls each of us to be good stewards of His gifts, so we should examine our lives and ask ourselves in what way are we sharing our time and talent as well as our treasure with the children of God. In the information to follow, I will use the term "Tithe" to refer to sharing of our treasure.

Tithing

A key component of my conversion story is how God revealed Himself in such a mighty way when I began to tithe my money. I have heard many a cynic say that tithing is something made up by preachers to fill the coffers at church. Others argue that in a country with a government such as ours, tithing is no longer necessary because much of our taxes are used to care for the needy.

What I have learned through my life experiences is that most people misunderstand why God calls us to tithe. Since God is all-powerful, do you really think He needs the money? Tithing isn't about God or even the people or organizations to whom we give. Tithing is about us and our relationship with God. I believe that tithing in its purest form removes the sense of individual ownership of anything by acknowledging that all we have belongs to God. With this in mind, whatever money I have belongs to us—meaning God and me. And God's promise to us all is that, when we acknowledge joint ownership of our money, He will pour out His blessing upon us.

While tithing is no more important than sharing our time and talent, it has been my experience that for most people, tithing is the most difficult. For some reason it is much easier to convince someone to give some of their time to help in a cause or use one of their talents such as singing than it is to ask them to give more than a dollar or two for a needy cause. I think it is because we place a higher premium on money than we do on our time and especially our talents. It is my theory that because this is so, God is quickest to respond when a person has the courage and humility to submit to God by acknowledging that all we have is His.

I promise that the stories I shared with you about God showing His helping hand when I began to tithe are only a few of the many, many ways He has kept His promise to me. In the twenty-five years since I began the practice of tithing I have shared my story with countless numbers of people, encouraging them to trust God with their money. I have sat with and counseled at least a dozen young couples over the years to help them get their finances in order, some of which were in pretty tough shape. In virtually every instance when the couple took the leap of faith and began trusting God with their money through tithing, they experienced astonishing results. With their permission I would like to share just a few stories from people who have chosen to trust God. For the sake of anonymity, with the exception of my children, I have changed the names of those whose stories I relate.

Story #1

During one of our parish council meetings at my church, I spoke to my fellow council members about the importance of tithing, asking that we be more active about teaching tithing to our parishioners. That evening I told the story I shared with you in Chapter 1 and asked that each member pray about what we, as a parish, should do.

In the parking lot after the meeting, one of the members of the council asked to speak with me. Jerry explained that he was touched by my story, but couldn't see how he could begin to tithe because he had been laid off from his job over a year before and was working at a much lower paying job, trying to get by while he continued looking for work. Jerry said he couldn't afford to give money away. Without hesitation I took Jerry by the hand, looked him in the eye, and said, "God is good for His word. Trust Him, and He will reward your trust."

A few months later Jerry stopped me again in the parking lot to tell me that when He got home that night after sharing my story and our conversation with his wife, Sharon, they decided that they would trust God. So they joined hands and prayed together, promising God they would trust Him, and from that day forward they would demonstrate their trust by tithing. The following week Jerry was hired to work at a job in his original field of experience at a salary level comparable to his salary before being laid off at a company which he had not applied until after they began tithing.

When seeking Jerry's permission to print his story, he

explained that in the years since we initially spoke, he and his wife have trusted God completely to lead them and have continued to tithe. In our conversation, Jerry explained that he didn't want people to think that tithing was some kind of trick or technique to "use" God. He said that he has just learned that if you really trust God, some pretty amazing things happen in your life. In our conversation Jerry told me, "I have no idea whether it is connected or not but, in June of this year my wife and I decided that it was time for me to retire, so we figured that I would do so in September. In late July my boss called me into his office to explain that the company was going through a reduction in force and that since I (Jerry) had the least seniority, I would be the one who would be let go. The end result was that I was able to retire one month earlier than we planned, but with a nice severance package!"

Jerry laughed and said, "We aren't rich by any stretch of the imagination, but there are times when we feel like we're members of the Gates family. The other day Sharon told me that our tithe account had built up to over $1,000 so we needed to make some decisions as to where it should go. It's such a wonderful feeling to be able to make a real impact in the life of someone in need."

Story #2

A young couple I worked with to help them get out of debt also committed to tithing. Phil and Marcia were the ones who drank the Super Big Gulps I spoke of, and most of their debt came from college student loans, expensive toys such as motorcycles and big screen TV's and jet skis. A couple months after they began tithing, Marcia's company offered stock options in lieu of cash bonuses that year. After the one year vesting period I advised Marcia to sell the options and use the profits to eliminate a significant portion of their debt. Only a few months after she did, the dot com bubble burst, and the value of the stock decreased dramatically.

Several years later Phil and Marcia, who were now parents of three boys, were living in Atlanta. By following my debt reduction program, they were in their early thirties with no debt except a small principle balance remaining on their mortgage. Phil was a computer guy, and Marcia was now, by choice, a stay-at-home mom when Phil became a casualty of the economic demise of many in the computer-related industry.

For the next eight years Phil was only sporadically employed, mostly through short-term consulting gigs or at best one year with one company. Yet, during that entire time they remained faithful to their tithing commitment. When I recently spoke with Phil, he explained that their trials seem to have ended, and Phil is once again gainfully employed by a stable company.

They were able to look back and say that they never went without, Marcia never had to work outside the home, and while they came "right to the edge," they never dipped into their permanent savings. Phil told me, "Those were scary times, but each time we thought we'd reached the end of our regular savings and would have to reach into our 'never-to-be-touched' account, another opportunity would come that would bring in enough income to keep us going. Had we been in debt, this would not have been possible. What we know without question is that if you trust God, He will not let you down."

It is also interesting to note that Phil told me that because he had worked with so many companies, his current boss considers Phil one of their biggest assets because of his broad spectrum of experience—experience that had been gained through the many, many assignments he had during the lean years.

Story #3

Near the end of this past school year I was walking to my car in the school parking lot when an elderly couple waiting in their car called my name. When I came over to them they smiled and told me that they talked about me a lot in their home. Since I was not teaching their grandson, who was a sophomore at my school, I was curious as to why. They explained that ten years ago they attended a seminar I conducted at church at which I discussed the very program I've shared with you. Bill and Mary, who are now in their seventies, shared with me that they decided after that seminar to do exactly what I taught. They immediately began to tithe, they read *Richest Man in Babylon*, did the cash flow analysis, and began executing their plan to completely eliminate their debt.

Just three months after the seminar, Bill's company began offering retirement packages to the employees who had been with the company a long time. It seems that it was financially better for the company to pay some pretty large exit packages to the higher paid employees to make way for the lower paid younger employees. Mary explained that since they had made the commitment to become completely debt-free, it was not a difficult decision to take the package which would pay off their remaining debt. She further explained, "While we didn't know what we would do after that, we trusted that God would help us figure that out."

Just a few months later, Mary's company also offered her an exit package to retire. Soon after they both retired, circumstances required that they care for two small children for several years, which Mary explained would not have been possible had they still been working full-time. We ended our conversation with Mary explaining that during this recession they have watched so many of their friends struggling to survive. Yet, because they are debt-free, even with the added financial burden of raising their grandson, whom they have since adopted, they wake up every morning stress-free knowing that God is with them.

Story #4

My daughter, Kathleen, and her husband, Adam, are adults who I believe epitomize what it means to walk confidently with God. From the day they got married I have marveled at the unflinching ways they demonstrate their trust in God. Theirs is not a rags-to-riches story, but a story of living with gratitude for the day and being content with the blessings they have.

After getting married in 2003, Adam accepted a graduate assistant position at Alfred University in western New York. At a school that had heated sidewalks because of the long, snowy winters, Kat and Adam lived in a school dormitory, in an expanded room configured for a single Residence Assistant. When Leslee and I went to visit them, we both were astonished at the way they were managing to live in this one bedroom apartment slightly bigger than our living room. Adam, who one year earlier was a 6′ 4″, 300 pound offensive lineman in a Division I football program, was sleeping in a bedroom slightly bigger than the *twin* bed, which was no more than 6′ long. Even while working in a school where several feet of snow is on the ground from Thanksgiving to Easter and drawing a monthly paycheck of less than $500, you would think that these two kids were living in paradise. And even with such a tiny salary, they faithfully gave 10% of their meager pay to those in need.

At the end of summer just before returning to Alfred, Kat and Adam were having dinner at our house. As desert was being served, they gave me a card congratulating me for being a new grandpa. While I was certainly excited about having my first grandchild, I did my best to hide how shocked and frightened I was for them. How were they ever going to afford a baby when Adam had another year of graduate school with next to nothing as a salary? Assuming that the baby was unexpected, I asked them if they were excited about the news. Adam was the first to speak up and explained that they were very excited and that they had planned the pregnancy. Kat told us that after much prayer and discussion, they felt they were ready to begin having children, and that if it was God's will also, they would trust Him to help them provide for their growing family.

If you are thinking that such talk was insane, think of what was going through my mind as I was looking at the happy faces of my children trying to hide the huge knot in my stomach. That night Leslee and I both said an earnest prayer thanking God for the gift of a new baby, but begging Him to honor the trust our kids were putting in Him.

With every nook and cranny of their car packed, the next morning Kat and Adam began their return trip to New York. About five hours after they left, we received a call from Kat asking if we would allow them to live with us for a while because Adam just received a phone call from UMBC, which is a university in Baltimore, offering Adam a full-time position in their athletic department. They literally turned around at an exit on the New Jersey Turnpike and came home!

Since then, Adam has changed jobs and is working for a hi-tech company and has been promoted to general manger. They have three children, live in a modest single family home just a few miles from us, and with every child Adam's salary has increased sufficiently enough to handle their increased need. It is a true blessing to observe them living the very things I am trying to teach in this book.

With these examples I want you to see that I'm not talking about some trick or gimmick to make you rich. These are stories of people who truly trusted God and, with that trust, have weathered some pretty tough financial trials. None are wealthy by the standards our society measures, but each are happy and content and sleep well at night knowing they are loved by God who is watching over them.

As I said at the beginning, God does not play favorites. We are all His children, and He wants to help us live fulfilled lives. The laws of God apply to everyone. Anyone who follows them will be blessed—even you.

How Does One Tithe?

Frequently people have questions about the details regarding tithing, such as where should they give their money, how much should they give, and is the percentage based on gross or net income? I think that if you are trying to calculate and justify the precise amount you give like you would an IRS tax return, your heart is not in the right place. I believe that at the core of tithing is one's relationship with God.

It bears repeating that tithing is not about the amount or the person or the entity receiving the gift. It is an outward manifestation of our trust in God. There are certainly people in this world, even in this country, who have no money to give. In the Gospel of Luke, the poor widow put two almost worthless coins in the temple coffer. When Jesus saw this He praised the woman for her love and trust in God, saying, "This poor widow put in more than all the rest; for those others have all made offerings from their surplus wealth, but she, from her poverty, has offered her whole livelihood." {Luke 21:3-4} God knows our hearts. It's not about how much—it's a matter of why. Having said this, there are still many who ask how I approach tithing in my life.

The Merriam-Webster Dictionary definition of the word *tithe* is to give a tenth of one's income. It also gives the etymology of the word as Middle English, from Old English *teogothian*, from *teogotha* meaning tenth. While

Stewardship ✳ 135

it has been my practice to give a least 10% of my gross income, I believe it is a matter of conscience between you and God. I've always tried to give as much as I could, but because of what I read in Malachi, I've considered 10% as my minimum.

When receiving any money, regardless of source, I take 10% of it and put it in a separate account that I can easily access through my checking account. Unlike other forms of savings, I do not set up a direct deposit with my employer for automatic deduction because I always want my giving to be a conscious thing. I believe, in doing so, I am continually reminded of my blessings, and I try to thank God each time I transfer money into the savings account. Therefore, throughout the year I have a pot of money that fluctuates in size.

The more frequent question is where to give the money. Once again I believe you should be led by the Spirit in this area. If you are a member of a church, then I think it is right to financially support the church that supports you. However, I have made it a practice to limit my contribution to no more than 5% of my income because I don't think it is healthy for any parishioner to exert too much influence on the pastor, whether financially or otherwise. I have a few charities that I pledge to support on an annual basis along with my church support, but there is always more money in the pot than required to fulfill those commitments. So, for the rest, I simply respond to requests that come my way as the spirit moves me. In this way, it is never a question of whether or not I should give; it is merely a question of to whom shall I give.

Time and Talent

I've decided to address the other two legs of the steward-ship stool together because it is difficult to separate the two. When you are giving your time, you are almost always using your talents while doing so. Just as with our money, every second of every day we live is but a gift from God—a gift we so easily take for granted. As a good steward, I think you should ask yourself how you are sharing your time with others. It's so easy to say that we are too busy, but I learned a long time ago if you really want something done, ask someone who is already busy. While it is possible to gain time by improving our time management skills, there does come a point when we simply do not have more time to give. We live in a seven-day-a-week world, and the concept of Sabbath rest has become almost a myth. So what can we do when we see ways we would like to help, but just don't have the time?

An important lesson I've learned is that when I am faced with a crisis or dilemma, a good place to start is on my knees, followed closely by seeking the answer to my prayers by reading the Bible. Jesus says in Luke, "Give and gifts will be given to you; a good measure, packed together, shaken down, and overflowing will be poured into your lap. For the measure with which you measure will in return be measured out to you." {Luke 6:38}

I've often heard this passage referred to as the law of sowing and reaping. In general, Jesus is telling us to give without counting the cost and, in doing so, God will take care of you. It certainly is the basis for the golden rule, but it is also so much more. Just like in Malachi, Jesus is saying that you will receive what you give, but when you give especially to those who can give nothing in return, God's blessings will be amazing.

So let's put this in farming terms (says the boy who grew up in the southwest desert). There is a farm down the street from my home where most years they plant corn. As I watch the farmer, it takes a few weeks to prepare the soil for planting. First he has to mow down the winter wheat, which I think is ultimately used for feed. He then plows the field, followed by planting the corn. In about a week we begin to see tiny green shoots popping through the ground, and after about six weeks it is astonishing to see these six-foot high corn stalks and on each stalk are five or six ears of corn. At harvest time the famer will cut down the stalks and pile up literally tens of thousands of ears of corn. Amazing!

Stepping back, let's examine this process. The farmer plows the soil, but the soil was made by God. The farmer plants the corn, but God made the corn. The corn is watered through the rain, which is provided by God, then the farmer cuts down the corn to sell in the market, keeping some to plant the following season. For the most part, no one really knows how that kernel of corn buried in the ground and dies becomes a corn stalk. But the miracle is that from one kernel of corn comes thousands and thousands of kernels of corn. As I see it, then, the vast majority of the farming process is completely dependent on God.

What Jesus is telling us in this passage is, you do the sowing, and God will do the growing.

This also means if you want corn, you need to plant corn, and when you do, you not only get corn, you get a whole lot more than you planted. So this is what I've found. If you don't have time to give to another, give it anyway because the law of sowing and reaping says if you give time, you'll get time back "packed together, shaken down, and overflowing." I promise when you trust God, nothing is impossible.

Why Does God Insist We Give?

In 2001 I went to Haiti for the first time at the request of a man who has become a dear, dear friend. In his wisdom, Dr. Rodrigue Mortel, a native Haitian, brought me to the place of his birth so I could experience first-hand the tragic existence of the people of Haiti. As Dr. Mortel had expected, that first visit changed my life forever.

When I looked into the eyes of a starving child lying in the arms of his starving mother, I realized I was looking directly into the eyes of Jesus and I heard my Lord plead with me saying, "Help me." I was haunted with questions. *Why was that child starving to death when I was overweight? Why was I born in this country with all its wealth and opportunity and these people born in dire poverty?* The only answer I could come up with was that while I cannot understand why, my circumstances in life are a gift from God—one that I must not waste.

It's so easy to look at the poverty in Haiti and ask why

God doesn't do anything about it. If He is so powerful, why does He allow such suffering? On this first visit to Haiti, the answer became clear to me in Jesus' words in chapter 25 of the Gospel of Matthew.

> 31 *When the Son of Man comes in his glory, and all the angels with him, he will sit upon his glorious throne,* 32 *and all the nations will be assembled before him. And he will separate them one from another, as a shepherd separates the sheep from the goats.* 33 *He will place the sheep on his right and the goats on his left.* 34 *Then the king will say to those on his right, 'Come, you who are blessed by my Father. Inherit the kingdom prepared for you from the foundation of the world.* 35 *For I was hungry and you gave me food, I was thirsty and you gave me drink, a stranger and you welcomed me,* 36 *naked and you clothed me, ill and you cared for me, in prison and you visited me.* 37 *Then the righteous will answer him and say, 'Lord, when did we see you hungry and feed you, or thirsty and give you drink?* 38 *When did we see you a stranger and welcome you, or naked and clothe you?* 39 *When did we see you ill or in prison, and visit you?* 40 *And the king will say to them in reply, 'Amen, I say to you, whatever you did for one of these least brothers of mine, you did for me.* 41 *Then he will say to those on his left, 'Depart from me, you accursed, into the eternal fire prepared for the devil and his angels.* 42 *For I was hungry and you gave me no food, I was thirsty and*

you gave me no drink, [43] *a stranger and you gave me no welcome, naked and you gave me no clothing, ill and in prison, and you did not care for me.* [44] *Then they will answer and say 'Lord, when did we see you hungry or thirsty or a stranger or naked or ill or in prison, and not minister to your needs?'* [45] *He will answer them, 'Amen, I say to you, what you did not do for one of these least ones, you did not do for me.'* [46] *And these will go off to eternal punishment, but the righteous to eternal life.* {Matthew 25:31-46}

Put simply, Jesus is telling us to get off our butts and do something about the inequities we see. World hunger is not caused by lack of food in the world. God has provided enough food on this earth to easily feed every human being with much to spare. The problem is distribution. People are starving because those who have the food are not willing to accept the responsibility for helping our fellow human beings on this planet who have nothing to eat.

The most glaring proof is that Haiti, the poorest country in the Northern Hemisphere, is less than 500 miles off the coast of the United States, the wealthiest nation in the world. Before you accuse me of oversimplifying, let me state that, having spent a great deal of time in Haiti attempting to bring some hope and assistance to those who live there, I am aware of the complexities of the issues that have brought about the situation in this nation. And giving them food is only a band aid. Actually fixing the problem is something that must come from within. But even in this case, Jesus is telling us to try, regardless of how hopeless something seems. With God, all things are possible. While working for change from within, do what you can to bring relief to those who are suffering.

Let's look beyond Haiti and consider again the above passage from Matthew. These words are straight-forward, not easily misunderstood. Jesus is telling us that God expects us to care for those in need. In the eyes of God, works of mercy are compulsory. Consider the last two verses when Jesus tells them if you ignored them, you ignored me, and "these will go off to eternal punishment." This warning takes on even greater significance when you consider that throughout the four Gospels, there are few times when Jesus is telling people do this or you are damned. Taken literally or figuratively, the point Jesus is making is that as members of the same human family, God is *compelling* all of us to help those who can't help themselves.

St. Teresa of Avila captured the essence of why we are called to serve others with this simple prayer:

Lord Christ,
You have no body on earth but ours,
No hands but ours,
No feet but ours.
Ours are the eyes through which your compassion
Must look out on the world.
Ours are the feet by which you may still
Go about doing good.
Ours are the hands with which

You bless people now.
Bless our minds and bodies,
That we may be a blessing to others. Amen

The more time I spent seeking God in my life, the more I longed to know Him and see His face. I often hear how difficult it is to have a relationship with someone you can't see. Because I agree with this statement, I challenge you to see for yourself what I have learned. If you really do want to see God, spend time with the poor, the aged, the sick, and the dying and look deeply into their eyes. These are God's precious. And, without question, where they are, so is He. There are no more powerful words in scripture to me than "when you did it to the least of these, you did it to me."

Like any relationship, building a close relationship with God takes time and effort. And in my thirty-three years of marriage I've learned that intimacy only comes from quality time together. When I began spending time with the poor and neglected, my relationship with God reached a level of intimacy I did not think possible.

PART 3

A New Beginning

Having addressed the pressing need and distraction of your financial stress, we turn now to what I believe is the most important part of this book. Even before Leslee and I had eliminated our debt, I began to feel a sense of calm and confidence because I had a plan that I knew, with God's help, would not fail. Because I didn't lie awake at night worrying about my finances anymore, my mind turned to the more important things in my life: my relationship with God, my relationship with my wife and children, and my real purpose in life. I am confident that if you will heed my advice in Part 2, you will also come to the same place.

With a renewed sense of hope, I believe that you will look at your life in a completely different light, asking yourself "what now?" This can be an exciting time for you as you begin your journey walking with God at your side. In this final section, I will address some of the questions and misgivings others and I have experienced as we consider ways of living a life that truly mattered and made a difference. It is my intent to give you things to think about as well as scripture passages to read that may help you focus your thoughts and prayers as you seek to find the answer to this question for yourself. In the end, the path you choose and the lives you touch will be a matter strictly between you and God.

8

Walking Confidently With God

Before I formed you in the womb I knew you.
JEREMIAH 1:5

Since I've used this expression several times and have chosen it as the title of this book, it's time that we focus our attention on what such a statement means to me and what it might look like for you. The challenge I face in attempting to define or even describe what it means to have confidence in God is akin to defining love. In fact, as I continued to consider ways to describe what I mean to walk confidently with God, I realized that to do so one must first delve into the substance of love.

The greeting card industry has made millions of dollars in helping people express their love, but how does one actually define love? When turning to the Webster's Dictionary I found more than ten attempts to define this simple four letter word. The first two definitions were: 1) strong affection for another arising out of kinship or

145

personal ties and 2) attraction based on sexual desire: affection and tenderness felt by lovers. Yet, one simply needs to observe the eighty-year-old man at the bedside of his dying wife of fifty-five years to see how far short these definitions fall from the mark. Or any parent would say how inadequate these words are when they hold their eight-year-old son in their arms after he's come home from school crying because the kids at school said he was stupid. While I would have argued on the day of my wedding that I loved Leslee more than I ever thought possible to love anyone, it was not until my children were born that I began to grasp the real meaning of love. It is from loving my children and watching my wife's love for them that my love for her grew even more. It is from loving my children that I began to grasp God's love for me and, with that awareness, my love for Him grew.

It becomes clear that much of one's understanding of love is based on experience, not intellectual exploration. The ancient Greeks had several words for the English word, love, one of which is *agape* (pronounced ah-gah'-pey). When using the word agape, the Greeks referred to a non-sexual love pertaining to the affection a parent had for a child or the affection two close friends would have for one another. In time, the early Christian Church began to use the term agape when referring to the selfless, self-sacrificing love of God toward His creation. Probably the most common depiction of agape love in the Catholic Church is the crucifix, which serves as a reminder of God's unconditional love through the sacrifice of His own son.

Because of the limitations of our human condition, it

is not possible for us to elicit agape love to the extent of our heavenly Father. However, each of us is made in the image of God our Creator, and as such, has the innate ability to evoke selfless love in our own unique way. I have come to realize that it is through the relationship between parent and child that we can best understand God's love for us. And it is in examining the bond between parent and child that I hope you will begin to see what it means to walk confidently with God.

While I admit that my understanding of agape love has been intensified by my experience as a father, most, to one extent or another, have experienced the selfless love of his or her own parents. However, even if not from one's biological parents such love could be exhibited by a teacher to a student, a coach to a player, and uncle to a niece or even between best friends. It is in the diversity of that personal experience between two people that makes it possible to begin to grasp the concept of confidence in God. I hypothesized in the prologue that trust is something learned over time and that trust comes from experience. And so it is with love. In fact, I believe that the basis for trust is love.

I have the wonderful opportunity to be a grandfather of five (so far). One of the best parts of being a grandparent is that I get to re-live the early days of my own parenthood, but as an observer and with the wisdom that can only come with age. As I watch the youngest of the grandkids I see them experience the agape love of their parents as they care for the child's every need. Even when caring for the infant means something as distasteful as dealing with a leaky diaper or a sick child who has vomited everywhere, I watch with pride as my children deal with the mess and care for their child in a completely selfless, loving manner.

However, it is in observing my four year old grand-daughter that I begin to see the response to the selfless love of a parent. Even at the early age of four, I listen to young Abby tell me with pride and confidence about all the things her Daddy can do. You can see in her eyes and hear in her words that there is no one stronger, smarter, or more competent than her Daddy. She sincerely believes that nothing bad could happen to her as long as her Daddy is there to watch over her.

When we would babysit Abby at the age of two, if something frightened her at night, the only ones who could really comfort her were her mom and dad. Yet, now that she is four, Grandma or Grandpa will do when she is scared or hurt—of course, only if Mommy or Daddy is not around. But by spending time with her, Abby has learned to trust her grandparents' love enough that we can fill in for her parents at least in a pinch. The point is that trust is built over time through getting to know someone and facing difficulties together.

Our grandchildren's love and confidence in their parents didn't just happen—it came from firsthand experience. Yet, another interesting observation I've made is that the younger siblings and even cousins seem to gain confidence quicker by watching and listening to the older kids. My son's oldest son, Tanner, is a kind and gentle little boy who is a bit standoffish and somewhat reticent around his more rambunctious cousins. Yet, the more time he spends with them, the more confidently he carries himself and the more willing he is to jump in and join in the fun. And in watching his cousins with their respective parents, Tanner becomes more comfortable and confident with his aunts and uncles.

As I watch my grandchildren, it becomes so obvious that love, trust, and confidence are all the product of experience. Because these experiences vary from one person to the next, the results can be both positive and negative. Not everyone has grown up in a loving, caring family. When someone violates our trust, it becomes more difficult to trust again. When we fail a few times, it becomes easier to believe we can't than to believe we can. Experience is an effective teacher.

In dealing with the concepts of love, trust and confidence I chose tangible examples to which we can all relate. Certainly for every example I provided, you could give me another dozen or more that are probably more effective and certainly more personal to you. Whether it is from the positive or negative viewpoint love, trust, and confidence are words I think most of us can grasp, at least from the tangible perspective. But does our understanding or, more important, our experience change when using these terms regarding our relationship with God?

How does one see God or experience God when He exists in spiritual realm? This is a complex question, one to which the answers would likely be extremely diverse. And therein is the conundrum. To walk confidently with God, one must first know that God is real. But knowing in your head is a long way from knowing in your heart. I think knowing in one's heart comes from experience. How can we experience the love of God like a child experiences the love of his or her parents? How can we experientially learn to trust God? Perhaps a more basic question would be, how do we get to know God if we can't spend time with Him? In the following pages I would like to suggest to you some ways that may help you find your own answers to these questions.

To Get to Know God, You Should Meet Him in the Scriptures

I am assuming that, because of its title, anyone who has chosen to read this book believes in God and, by this point in the book, at least hopes that what I've said is true and is applicable to themselves. I believe that the personal life experiences of each reader will make it easier or harder to accept the premise that God loves them and wants a close, intimate relationship with them right here and now. The good news is that regardless of your previous experience, you can begin anew.

In some ways, I think the greater challenge may come to the seasoned Christian who has worked hard to live their life according to what he or she has learned to be the *teachings of the church*. All my life, I've been what some may call a devout Catholic. While many choose to stray from their faith, especially in their adolescent and early adult years, I have always remained faithful to my Catholic practices. In my case, my professed belief and my actions contradicted each other. Without a doubt, I believed in God and was quite content with my beliefs and faith practices. It took near disaster in my life to shake me from my complacency and help me get to know God just as I knew my earthly father. And just as with my earthly father, getting to know God came from experience. And so it will be for you.

While I now can see many, many ways that God was actively involved in my life when I was younger, the first time I recognized God's loving hand in my life was when I met John. Yet, it was not until I was so desperate and broken that I realized how much I needed Him. And after I took that leap of faith, I seemed to recognize Him all around me. Tithing was simply my act of faith, my response to God's plea to come to Him. God's dramatic response, once I pledged to trust Him, was His way of encouraging me to get to know Him better. Yet, while I was conscious of God's existence and loving assistance, it was not until I started to read the Bible that I began to get to know Him on a much more personal level.

While in high school my youngest daughter, Maureen, had a group of friends over at our house frequently. These kids often got into some pretty interesting debates about various topics, including things they were studying in their scripture classes at school. In one heated discussion I heard one young lady tell the group that her father taught her that "faith is not belief without reason; it is trust without reservation." She was an extremely bright young lady who has since gone on to law school and, during these debates, I often watched Laura challenge the premise of accepting things simply on faith.

It was interesting to watch this aspiring young lawyer challenge her schoolmates yet, while doing so, her study and debate deepened her own conviction in her trust in God. She once told me that the more she read the New Testament, the more she wanted to read it. She was fond of asking me if I had any idea how powerful it was to read about Jesus yourself and not just to listen to someone else explain it. While indeed I did know, I have found that the only way to grasp such a declaration is to discover it for yourself.

I suggest, then, as you take the leap of faith and prove your trust in God by tithing, and at the same time, begin to read the Bible. It is in reading the word of God for yourself that God reaches out and touches you. Often I have found the answers to my prayers or conclusions to important decisions came when reading scripture. While there are many support books written that will help you read and understand the Bible, perhaps you can begin by approaching your pastor, rabbi, or imam, or a friend that you know who reads scripture regularly and ask for his help in getting started.

I am frequently asked which Bible one should read. Because of my graduate work, I personally own nine different translations of the Bible and have referred to them all at different times during my studies. However, the Bible I read every day is the St. Joseph's edition of the New American Bible mainly because it is the translation from which the readings are taken at a Catholic Mass. It is also the Bible from which I teach in school.

While biblical scholars will argue the accuracy of the various translations from the original texts, I think that the most important aspect of the Bible for the lay person is that it is one that you will actually read. From a practical perspective, if you belong to a church, it would be helpful to use the translation that the rest of the congregation uses, especially if you gather for Bible study. Of course, if you are Jewish I encourage you to spend time reading the Tenach and especially the Torah. While the Talmud and Mishna are important support texts, I urge you to read the word of God yourself. And to my Muslim brother or sister, I also encourage you to not only read the Qur'an, but to expand your reading to the Hebrew and Christian Scriptures.

My message is simple. To get to know God, you should meet Him in the Scriptures. If you are having a difficult time reading the Bible you have, look at a few of the student Bibles available which include easy to understand explanations and are written to assist a lay person in his/her journey through scripture.

Why Would God Bless Me?

A common challenge people face when beginning this journey of trust is battling a sense of misgiving or unworthiness. Especially because God's response in my life was so quick and generous, I was initially filled with uneasiness. I could not understand why God would be so good to me. After all I had done to mess up our finances, moreover after the way I treated Leslee and the kids, there was no way I deserved to be blessed the way God was blessing me.

When I shared with John the feelings I was having, he, once again, led me to scripture to find my answer. Just as John directed me, I ask you to read Chapter 15 of the Gospel of Luke. In this chapter Jesus tells the parable of the prodigal son. While the parable is about the lost son, the lesson of the parable is all about the father. Jesus is giving us yet another glimpse of how much God loves us and wants us to be with Him.

A subtle but powerful component of this parable is when the son returns after squandering all his inheritance. Jesus says, "While he was still a long way off, his father caught sight of him, and was filled with compassion. He ran to His son, embraced him and kissed him." {Luke 15:20} The reason the father sees his son while he was "a long way off" was because he was looking for him. The mental image I have when reading this passage is this distraught old man praying every day for the wellbeing of his wayward son. Each day the man searches the horizon hoping that his son will return to him safely. Then Jesus says as soon as the father sees him, he runs to the boy. When reading this, I realized that Jesus is telling me that when I was feeling so stressed, struggling with my finances and acting horribly with my family, God was worried about me and was just waiting for the opportunity to help. And just as the man in the parable ran to his son, as soon as I made a move back in God's direction, He ran to my aid.

If you're feeling unsure that God wants to help you, read Chapter 15 in Luke. Of course we're not worthy of God's love! Of course we've all messed up! But that doesn't matter to God. God made us because He loves us and wants us to be happy. He wants us to be with Him. We need only to turn His direction and ask for help.

Another misgiving that people have shared with me is

their sense of ineptness. I certainly felt like a total failure because I was so careless with our money. And then I had to admit that I didn't know how to get out of the mess I was in. However, others have said to me that they could see how I could recover quickly because I was a Naval Academy graduate, had a very successful Navy career, and lots of experience that helped me develop my new career. Their concern is that they didn't graduate from college and have limited skills or experience, and there is nothing they can do to improve themselves. To respond to this misgiving I shall follow the example of my friend, John, and refer you to scripture. This time I ask you to go to the Gospel of John at the beginning of Chapter 6 where John describes the multiplying of the loaves and fish. It is interesting to note that this event was so significant that it is the only miracle described in each of the four Gospels.

In this story Jesus was in a remote area, far from any town, and thousands of people had come to listen to Him preach. When Jesus saw such a large crowd, he was worried that they would go hungry, so He wanted to feed them. Andrew told Jesus that there was a boy among them who had five loaves of bread and two fish. From that small amount of food Jesus fed the multitude.

While there is so much that can be learned from every story in scripture, there are two lessons from this story that address the concerns of feeling inept. First, the people did not come to Jesus complaining they were hungry. They came wanting to learn from Him. Jesus knew they would be hungry, and He wanted to feed them. So, too, does God know what we need and is anxious to help us. Second, Jesus was able to take the small amount of food they had and easily feed all who were with Him.

I believe Jesus would tell you not to worry about what kind of education you have or what skills and abilities you have. God is God, for goodness sake. He will take whatever we have and work with that. Just look at the apostles. Jesus picked twelve guys who were uneducated, unsophisticated, total cowards, and who most often were completely clueless. Yet, after being filled with the Holy Spirit, these men became bold and articulate and fearlessly preached the Good News of Jesus. With God by their sides, the apostles accomplished amazing things before all but John willingly suffered torturous deaths for the sake of the Gospel.

Just trust God and bring to Him what you have, and let Him do the rest.

What Does God Want Me to Do With My Life?

The more we were able to bring our finances under control and the better I got to know God, the more discontent I became with myself. Just as children strive to please their parents and want to make them proud of their accomplishments, I too, wanted to please God. My Heavenly Father had given me so much that I desperately wanted to use the gifts He had given me to accomplish great things for Him. I so often heard people say that God has a plan for each person's life and, thus, became preoccupied pondering this possibility. My questions were: Does God really have a plan for us all? If so, what was God's plan for me? What if what I was doing had nothing to do with God's plan for me? If I weren't doing what God had intended, was He going to be upset with me? How could I even do the things He wanted me to do unless He told me His plan?

In exasperation I would say, "I just wish God would show me what He wants me to do." How often has that wish crossed your mind? It sure seems like life would be so much simpler if we knew with certainty what God wanted for us. I've often said that in some ways, it is harder for us than Moses or the other prophets, because they actually got to hear God's voice. I think that if I knew without a doubt that God was telling me to do something, I wouldn't hesitate to do it. It's the not knowing that makes things difficult.

This, however, raises an interesting and profound question. Does God actually have a plan for us? I believe the answer to this question is a pivotal component in understanding our relationship with God and is essential in helping you walk confidently each day with Him. I, for one, wrestled with this question for nearly thirty years beginning when I was a senior in high school.

When I was a young boy, I was strongly influenced by my mother whose fervent prayer was that I would grow up to be a priest. By the time I was in the fourth grade, my mother had made me a set of vestments so I could *play* Mass. Both my mother and father instilled in me a deep love for Jesus and often spoke of how God calls people to His service. Yet, outside my family, I was seen as a kid who was outspoken, got into mischief frequently, excelled in football, dated regularly, and to more people than I would like to admit, was considered too cocky for my own good.

It was common practice in Catholic Schools in the sixties to administer vocation aptitude tests to high school seniors. These tests served as indicators of kids who would do well in a religious vocation. After taking one of these tests, I was called into a meeting with the school principal where the test administrators told me that I had scored extremely high. These men had explained to my principal that I should seriously consider entering the seminary to become a priest. Because of my outward persona, my principal, Brother Stephen, assured the gentlemen that the results had to be in error. Much to Brother Stephen's relief, I agreed with my principal and told the men that I had no intention of becoming a priest. Yet, inside, my stomach was churning as I silently agonized over that conversation.

Three years later, while at the Naval Academy, I had many long and emotional discussions with one of the chaplains, questioning whether or not God was calling me to the priesthood. Yet, when I went home for the Easter holidays that year and spent time with my eight brothers and sisters as well as all my nephews and nieces, I told myself, "I don't care if God wants me to be a priest. I want to be a dad."

Even once I met Leslee and knew she was the one with whom I wanted to share the rest of my life, I struggled with this worry that I was running from God. And so to reassure myself that I was doing the right thing, I asked three of my closest friends as well as two adults, all of whom knew me as well as Leslee, if they thought I should marry or become a priest. From each the answer was the same; "I think you should be a priest." Once again, though, I rejected their response to marry the woman I loved.

For years after we married I lived with a quiet sense of guilt that I had told God no to selfishly follow my heart. In fact, when we were told we should get a divorce, the first thought that came to my mind was "That's what I get for defying God!" I actually began to think that my marital and financial struggles where God's punishment for running from Him.

So let's step back and examine my emotional conclusion from the perspective of a loving parent. Does it make any sense that a parent who truly loves his child would try to ruin that child's life just because he chose a career you didn't approve of or marry a person you didn't like? Of course not.

Thus, I've concluded that God must know the best path for us to take in life, but regardless of how wonderful or important that path may be, He will never compel us to follow it. God is not a puppeteer pulling strings making each of us dance. More than anything else, God wants us to be happy. Yet it has taken me fifty six years to realize that true happiness comes in service to others. So if we choose to do something that takes us on a path different than God would have chosen, He is ready to help us make the best of our journey along that path. We need only ask.

To all who spend countless hours worrying about the future, I think God might tell you to take a deep breath and relax. Jesus said it succinctly when he said, "Do not worry about tomorrow; tomorrow will take care of itself." {Matt 6:34} The problem is we want God to show us our future, yet the reality is our future is fluid, completely determined by decisions we make every day. Psalm 119 verse 105 gives us a hint when the writer says: "Your word is a lamp for my feet, a light for my path."

God wants us to live in the present and make the most of what we have. We need to recognize that each moment we live is a gift that we should cherish. The message Jesus gave us is that we are not alone in our decisions. Regardless of what path we choose, God is by our side. If we choose to let Him, God will help us in our choices.

I recognize that each person reading this book is at a different place in their belief and/or relationship with God. The good news is God recognizes that also. He loves you just as you are and wants you to know that. He didn't select me over you or anyone else. He will meet you where you are now and will help you in ways that you are ready to handle.

Walking confidently with God means trusting that God is with you every day, whether you are weak and broken or strong and confident. And as you begin to experience His loving hand in response to your trust, you will learn to recognize him in the voices and faces of the people around you just as you recognize the voice of a close friend when she speaks on the telephone. My prayer each day is that I realize when He is trying to get my attention, for I have found that when I am in complete sync with my Heavenly Father, life is really good. And when I stop listening or try to ignore Him, life tends to get pretty complicated. To illustrate this, let me tell you one last story when God tried to speak to me through my son.

Several years after we had completely eliminated our debt, my son Matthew had a heart to heart talk with me. He wanted to know how much money was enough. His question threw me and I asked why he was asking. He explained that I was working so much that I never seemed to have enough time to spend with him or his sisters. In his innocent wisdom, Matt explained that now that he was starting high school, it was important that I was around to be at his ball games and involved in his life. And since I frequently explained to my kids that I was gone a lot because I was earning money to support them and provide for their future, Matt simply wanted to know when I would have enough money to not be away so much.

His line of questioning gave me great pause. Because I was a self employed consultant, my income was a function of the number of hours I worked. Back then, it was not unusual for me to bill 3,000 hours in a year which meant that there were many weeks when I worked eighty plus hours. What my teenage son was lovingly telling me was, "Pop, you've gotten confused. We need *you* more than your money." In this case, I have no doubt God was speaking through Matt. Even though I did recognize God's hand, I really didn't get the full meaning of His message. While I did make some changes that allowed me to spend more time with my wife and kids, it would be almost ten more years before I really acknowledged that I was traveling the wrong path for me.

My entire life I have felt that God has been calling

me to serve Him in a special way. Even though I made it very clear that I was not going to be a priest, I continually sought ways to serve God. While on sea duty in the Navy, I served as a lay chaplain aboard a destroyer and was active in lay ministry aboard an aircraft carrier. When I first left the Navy, I tried to serve in my parish in various ways, but as business increased and I assumed a senior leadership role at FTI, I found I no longer had time to give.

I justified my lack of giving personal time with the amount of money I gave to churches and charities and kept promising myself and God that when I retired, I would dedicate the majority of my time to serving God as He directed me. As a key player in building a rapidly growing public company, I kept telling myself that in just a couple more years my net worth would be sufficient to retire, and then I would serve God. Because I was overseeing the opening of a major office in Manhattan, for over a year I was living in an apartment in New York and coming home to my family two to three weekends a month.

One Thursday evening I received a phone call from Leslee asking me to come home that night because she needed to have emergency surgery the next morning to remove a massive tumor the doctors discovered in her uterus. Because of its rapid growth and overall size, the doctors felt it was likely the tumor was malignant. After a surgery which took almost two hours longer than anticipated, a difficult time recovering from the anesthesia, followed by three days which felt like a lifetime, the doctors came back with the report that the tumor was benign. They explained that they were so sure the tissue was malignant that they ordered a second biopsy to confirm the findings of the first test. There was no sign of cancer anywhere!

Finally, after this terrifying experience, Matt's words came back to me: "How much money is enough?" Leslee and I spent our time in the hospital talking about what was important in life to each other, and what we both realized was that once again we were allowing money to be a stumbling block toward our peace. Because we had been in such debt with absolutely nothing in savings, I had let the pendulum swing the other direction. I wanted to make sure we would never digress. So I worked constantly with the mindset of *just a little more.* I was not trusting God and He knew it.

Recognizing my mistake, I turned to the wisdom of Jesus as related in the Gospel of Luke. I find it particularly ironic that over fifteen years after that horrible yet awesome night when I clearly heard God's voice speaking to me, asking me to walk confidently with Him, that I would once again hear the same encouraging words in the paragraph immediately preceding the words I read as a broken, frightened young man.

> 16 *Then he told them a parable, "There was a rich man whose land produced a bountiful harvest.* 17 *He asked himself, 'What shall I do, for I do not have space to store my harvest?'* 18 *And he said 'This is what I shall do: I shall tear down my barns and build larger ones. There I shall store all my grain and other goods* 19 *and I shall say to myself 'Now as for you you have so many good things stored up for many years, rest, eat,*

drink, be merry.' " 20 But God said to him, 'You fool, this night your life will be demanded of you; and the things you have prepared, to whom will they belong?' 21 Thus will it be for the one who stores up treasure for himself, but is not rich in what matters to God. {Luke 12:16-21}

For years I shared my story with many people encouraging them to trust God, especially with their money. Over and over again I told people that God is worthy of our trust, yet my actions certainly contradicted my words. The reality is that the same sense of pride that kept me from turning to God for help so many years ago was now keeping me from acknowledging that the blessings I had were gifts from God. He helped me in the past and was certainly going to continue helping me in the future. The fact was, I had gotten used to making lots of money. My hesitancy to leave was my lack of trust in God and my growing attachment to money.

So in 2001, I chose to once again leap into God's arms. Four months after Leslee's surgery I resigned my position as president, leaving behind a significant income during a time when the company was on the verge of becoming a multi-billion dollar entity. And for the next three years I did everything I could think of to serve God. While pursuing a masters in theology, I was making trips to Haiti, managing the facilities of my parish as a volunteer, leading the parish building campaign both in fund-raising and design and much more. But nothing I did seemed to satisfy me or bear fruit.

As part of my graduate work in theology, I was on a weekend retreat which began with a meeting with my professor, who was a feisty old nun and a delight to be with. She was to serve as my spiritual director during the retreat and asked what I would like to focus on over the weekend. I told her that I was having difficulty focusing at all because I was not very happy with God at the time. I explained that for three years I was running myself ragged doing everything I could for God and had no clue what He wanted me to do. So in frustration I said I just wish He would pick one of these things and let me know which one.

After thinking for a few moments her response was, "While I don't know how God would answer, if I were God, I would say 'who the hell do you think you are, giving me a list of things to choose from! I'll tell you what, why don't you sit on the bench for a while, and I'll let you know if I think I can use you.'" Her blunt response certainly got my attention. After spending the weekend thinking and praying about her words, I concluded that she was right. Who did I think I was? So after returning from my retreat, I spent the next month resigning from all my commitments, including suspending my graduate studies. I told Leslee it was time to relax and play golf.

A couple months later, just three days before Leslee and I were leaving for a golf trip in Florida, I received a phone call from the principal of my kids' high school asking if I would consider covering the classes of a religion teacher who had just quit. When I met with the principal, I explained that while I was confident in the subject matter, I was unsure of dealing with high school students. So she suggested I observe a class in session to get a sense of what it would be like.

Sitting in that classroom watching the teacher explain the meaning of God's word in scripture, I knew instantly I would do it and couldn't wait to get started. After I accepted, the principal asked if I was sure, to which I responded "No, but I'm sure available." It seemed to me that the God was turning to the bench and sending me into the game. And as I begin my sixth year during which I will spend nine months sharing my faith and listening to the questions and ideas of my students, I can only marvel at the wisdom of my Father. These have been some of the most fulfilling and stress free years of my life.

Leslee frequently jokes that when looking to the future, I'm always thinking in grandiose ways of how I might change the world. But for now, I think God is asking me to humble myself and help Him reach out and touch the hearts of high school seniors. And perhaps, by the grace of God, one of them will change the world!

Perhaps the most succinct way I can summarize my message is to say that God knows what is best for you, but even when you strayed from the path he had in mind, He will never give up on you. And because I learned to trust Him, things have turned out better than I could have ever dreamed. So what about you? Are you ready to place you trust in God?

9

Are You Ready to Leap?

. . . be renewed in the spirit of your minds, and put on the new self, created in God's way in righteousness and holiness of truth.

EPHESIANS 4:23-24

The purpose of all my stories in Part 1 was to show you why I believe you can live a life completely free of debt or financial stress. My message has been simple. Just as God has blessed me, He will bless you if you trust Him and put Him first in your life. Part 2 gave you a simple method to conquer your debt, change your buying mindset, and effectively use the money you earn. Then, with your finances under control, I spoke of ways that will help you stay out of debt and focus on the important things in life.

Yet all of this was with the hope that, like me, you will discover that the reason for your financial troubles, your relationship problems, or your feelings of discontent are spiritual and not financial. I was in debt to many people, both financially and emotionally, because I was not indebted to God for the amazing gifts He had given me. But that did not have to remain so. Neither does it have to remain for you. The question is, are you ready to let go and let God?

Through prayer, studying the Bible, and my graduate work in theology, I have come to believe that God created the universe for us (the human race), and He created us to be His companions. He wasn't looking for slaves or toys. God created us in His image to be his family. However, because His most significant gift to us was that of free will, out of pride we have chosen to turn from God, thinking that we can go it alone. And it is because of our stubborn pride that the world is as messed up as it is. Yet there is hope.

> [16] *For God so loved the world that he gave his only Son, so that everyone who believes in him might not perish, but might have eternal life.* [17] *For God did not send his Son into the world to condemn the world, but that the world might be saved through him.* [18] *Whoever believes in him will not be condemned, but whoever does not believe has already been condemned because he has not believed in the name of the only Son of God.* [19] *And this is the verdict that the light came into the world, but the people preferred darkness to light, because their works were evil.* [20] *For everyone who does wicked things hates the light and does not come toward the light, so that his works might not be exposed.* [21] *But whoever lives the truth comes to the*

light so that his works may be clearly seen as done in God. {John 3:16-21}

This is such a popular passage that it is often referred to as the *football* verse because it is frequently seen on national TV when the cameras pan the crowd and someone has "John 3:16" written on a poster as a means of evangelization. But let us not dismiss this passage as a mere slogan. The temptation when reading this passage is to jump to the most obvious and deal with this incredibly powerful revelation only on the surface.

For many, the *church* seems focused on sin and damnation. Catholics have made a science of the many ways we feel guilty about the ways we are "bad" in the eyes of God. To some, life is a testing ground that determines whether we go to Heaven or Hell when our life comes to an end. Many will hone in on verse 18 feeling that this is a key element of the Christian faith. Verse 18 seems to clearly state that unless we "believe in him," we will be condemned to hell. But is that really what John is trying to tell us?

Before I delve further let me reiterate that Jesus wants us to think of God in the way we see our human father. Our Daddy loves us and would never do anything to hurt us on purpose. He wants us to be happy and will try his best to help us. So, "if you then, who are wicked, know how to give good gifts to your children, how much more will your heavenly Father give good things to those who ask him?" {Matthew 7:11}

As I look back at the many years during which I have

watched my kids grow into amazing adults, I remember
times that they did things that were dumb and even at
times dangerous. While most of the time they were kind,
loving, generous, and fun to be with, there were times
when they were selfish, petty, spiteful, and mean. But no
matter how they behaved, I've always loved them more
than I thought would be possible to love anyone. When
they were young and I had to discipline them in some way,
it was so difficult to watch them cry and not scoop them
up into my arms and tell them how much I loved them.
When they were angry with me because I said no to a
request, or did something that embarrassed them, I was
hurt and wanted nothing more than to make things right.

Now that they are grown with families of their own,
I have made it my practice to never offer any unsolicited
advice. And because of that decision, there are times when
I have had to watch them make mistakes that have given
them heartache. Because we are pretty close as a family, there have also been times when my kids have done
things that they have consciously and carefully tried to
keep from me for fear that I would not approve. What is
difficult for them to grasp, and for me to express, is that
the only thing that really matters is that they know that I
love them unconditionally. Certainly there have been times
when I have been angry with them, and even times when
I did not like what they were doing but I always have and
always will love them and will do anything I can to help
them be happy.

If I, as a weak and limited human being, am capable
of such feelings for my children, how much more must

God care about us? So what was the message Jesus died trying to tell us? Quite simply He told us that God loves us more than any parent on earth could love his child, and He desperately wants to spend eternity with us. Through His eternal wisdom, God knows what will make us happy, but like so many rebellious teenagers, we refuse to listen. We refuse to accept the possibility that He knows what is best for us and is trying to lead us in that direction. The older I get, the more I recognize how little I really know. Young children inherently know that their parents know more than them and trust their parents to make good decisions for them. And from fifty-six years of experience, I have concluded that it takes wisdom to acknowledge our ignorance regarding the ways of God and faith to accept His help. I believe St. Paul said it best when he wrote "If God is for us, who can be against us?" {Romans 8:31}

If His message is so simple and the reward so great, why do we fight it? I believe there are primarily two reasons: *selfishness* and *pride*. Selfishness hinders us because we think that if we do accept this whole idea of God, then we will be limited in what we can do. To many, God represents a whole bunch of thou shalt nots! Many think that if they live their life with and for God, they will live a boring life with lots of hours spent in Church and in prayer and not doing the fun things. I hear my students say all the time that someday they are sure they will get serious about religion, but for now God is not that important to them. After all, they have a pretty good life and are certainly having lots of fun, so they don't need Him.

I believe that this reasoning reaches way beyond the

high school kids I teach and way beyond the teenage years. There are many adults today living with the intention of one day taking this religion stuff more seriously. They are spending so much time chasing the *good life* that they are missing the opportunity to live a *great life* with God.

The second stumbling block is that of pride. For some, believing in God and especially depending on God, is a sign of weakness. They think I *have a keen intellect and have the ability to reason my way through life.* Even if they do believe that God exists, they certainly don't need His help.

I had one particular student in my "Christian Spirituality" class, who displayed an amazing intellect and seemed to ponder the bigger issues of life more than most her age. In a reflection paper she wrote at the beginning of the semester, Kelly explained that the more she learned about science, the more she realized that if God exists at all, He certainly wasn't a key figure in her life. She felt that religion in general was for the weak and unnecessary for anyone willing to seek answers through science. With her permission, I would like to share with you the observations of this amazing young woman. By way of explanation, her references to her time in chapel are speaking of a practice I had of taking the kids to our school chapel once a week to give them an opportunity to sit quietly and just "be" with God.

> The best part of this class was the time we spent in the chapel. It amazes me still what wonders forty-five minutes of time for only God and myself can do. By simply sitting silently and really thinking

about what I believe, it was so much easier than I ever thought it would be to begin to understand my faith. At first, it amazed me how little I really knew about my faith. I knew the book knowledge. I've always been an avid reader in any area. What I didn't know was what I really thought about it all. I'd always assumed that 'faith' was a crutch for the weak, and that 'strong' people did not need faith. I've come to see things a little bit differently now. From what I've learned about myself, I do not need faith to get through my day. I can sleep at night without it. However, what I believe is that all people need faith to make necessary changes in our troubled world. God is a crutch for the weak. But how can a man with a broken leg ever learn to walk again without using his crutch? He must lean on it in his time of need until he has the strength to walk forward on his own legs. However, in the same breath, the strong still need God. The strong man must still appreciate what the crutch did for him in his time of need and what it will do in the future when he unwittingly hurts himself again. Even more important, when a weak person has been hurt, either by his or her own doing or by something completely out of his or her control, such as poverty or sickness, the strong man must have the crutch to share, to better the weak. In this way, God is always necessary, and it is not a bad thing to be weak and need God's care. All of us are weak in the face of the harsh realities of life and must appreciate the great gift of the crutch God gives us to make it through the tough times. God's love will lift us up, even when we cannot stand on our own. This I began to understand while meditating in the chapel, and I am thankful for the opportunity to realize these things.

(KELLY MANN, ARCHBISHOP SPALDING
HIGH SCHOOL CLASS OF 2009)

I challenge you to consider the profound words of this eighteen-year-old girl. "All of us are weak in the face of the harsh realities of life," so why let pride stand in your way? Why not allow God to help you in all things in your life, including your finances? He wants you to be happy. He doesn't want you to live a stressful life. So what's stopping you from trusting God?

To better understand our hesitancy, let us consider the spider monkey. In many areas of South America spider monkeys are popular as pets. They are affectionate and appear to be quite intelligent. They are quick and agile, which should make capturing them uninjured quite difficult. The operative word here is *should,* because understanding the ways of these monkeys, the people living in the South American jungles have devised an ingenious and almost effortless way of capturing this seemingly elusive creature.

The process begins by hollowing out a gourd with a bulbous body and long narrow neck. Inside the gourd the hunter places some type of food especially attractive to spider monkeys. Then they tie a rope securely around the neck of the gourd. They then go into the forest and tie the other end of the rope to a tree in an area where spider monkeys live.

When a monkey smells the food in the gourd, it will make its hand as skinny as possible to slide down the neck of the gourd. However, once it grasps the food, the monkey's hand is now in the shape of a fist which is too large to fit through the neck of the gourd thereby making it stuck. So the only way to get his hand out of the gourd would be to let go of the food. Yet the monkey will not relinquish his prize.

The screams and cries of the monkey with his fist stuck in the gourd tied to a tree acts as an alarm to alert the captors that their trap has done its job. They simply return to the trap, untie the rope from the tree, and walk the screaming monkey back to their camp as if the monkey were on a leash. To avoid capture the monkey simply had to let go of the food. Yet, it seems the food in hand was more important than freedom.

I'm not sure that story is true, but you get the analogy.

So what is your "monkey food"? What are you holding onto so tightly that it is preventing you from real change? Once again, I challenge you to be brutally honest and ask yourself what is holding you back. I used to dismiss as a mere platitude the expression "let go and let God," yet therein lays the rub. Why won't you ask God for help? Why don't you want to believe that He can and/or will help you? Why won't you turn to others for help? Is it pride? Is it stubbornness? Is it fear? Whatever the reason, I beg you to let go.

My life changed in an amazing way the day I decided

to take God at His word and trust Him with my life. In so many ways God has proven His trustworthiness to me. So why not put Him to the test? To some, testing God may even sound like blasphemy, but I assure you I have scripture to support my challenge. I think that money is so important to all of us that trusting anyone with our money represents the height of trust. I challenge you to allow God to show Himself to you. When speaking about tithing in the book of Malachi, God says, "Bring the whole tithe into the storehouse, that there may be food in my house, *and try me in this,* says the Lord of hosts, Shall I not open for you the floodgates of heaven and pour down blessings upon you without measure?" {Mal 3:10} The way I would paraphrase this is "I dare you to test me. Give me the first fruits of your labor and watch me shower you with blessing."

I so want you to experience how wonderful life can be when lived without stress walking with God at your side. More important, God wants it for you. I said at the very beginning that trust is something that takes practice. So commit to follow the suggestions I have given you, especially if you are in debt, and start tithing today. It's not magic; it's trust. Be willing to work every day like it all depends on you and pray every night like it all depends on God. It is my most sincere prayer that you will open your heart to His love and that you experience the amazing life that comes from walking confidently with God.

Acknowledgements

Writing a book for the first time has proven to be both challenging and rewarding. Without a doubt, this adventure in writing, rewriting, building up, and dismantling the flow and structure of the message, would not have been as fruitful nor as meaningful without my loving family's help.

Thank you so much Matt, Mel, Kat, Adam, Maureen, Tom, Dave and Leslee, my sweet wife. Your love and commitment to ensure that I got it right came at the expense of your valuable free time. I knew you all meant business when Matt began our first feedback session with "I hope you're not looking for fluff!" That night, when Adam asked me if I was okay, I told him I was feeling a little overwhelmed. However, I shared with Leslee later that I was actually overcome with emotion because everyone's willingness to help showed me how truly blessed I am. Thank you all for loving me in spite of all my flaws.

Tom, your tireless efforts to read page after page of re-writes goes way beyond the call of family commitment and certainly earned you many *favorite-son-in-law* points. I've become so dependent on you filling the role of managing editor, that I'm nervous about including this section without your insightful review. So, Tom, if there are errors in this, you and I will know why.

I want to thank Leslee. You have been my partner

through all our stories as well as my writing about them and have done so with patience and grace. Thank you for hanging in there with me.

Finally, I want to thank John for being the answer to my prayers. Your love, friendship, and Godly example were the instruments God chose to rescue me.

I pray that God will use our collective efforts to turn the hearts of those in need.

Learn More

To learn more about the principles discussed in
Walk Confidently With God visit our website:
www.patrickabrady.com

▶ Download helpful tools to:
  • Track your daily spending
  • Develop a budget
  • Track and evaluate your budget
▶ Watch short videos discussing money
  management concepts/techniques
▶ Find links to helpful sites pertaining to money
  management and spiritual growth
▶ Communicate with the author
▶ Purchase additional copies of *Walk Confidently
  With God*

For information about having the author speak
to your organization or group contact us at
bradyspeak@verizon.net

The Kids in Haiti Need Your Help

 In January 2002 I traveled to Haiti for the first time. My dear friend Dr. Rodrigue Mortel, who is a native Haitian, asked me to come with him to experience firsthand the plight of his fellow countrymen. From the moment I arrived, I realized that I was not prepared for what I would see and experience over the next few days. My first experience was overwhelming leaving me with sense of urgency to help in some way.

While it is only 500 miles off the coast of Florida, Haiti is the poorest country in the Northern Hemisphere. The abject poverty of her citizens is all pervasive. So much that one out of every five children in Haiti will never reach the age of five. However, in spite of their circumstances, I have found the people of Haiti to be warm and hospitable and grateful for the assistance they receive from Americans.

Since my first visit I have returned many times and have been doing whatever I can to help raise awareness of God's precious poor in Haiti. Through the leadership of Dr. Mortel, we have been able to build a wonderful elementary school called Les Bons Samaritains (The Good Samaritans

School). Because our school has been extremely success-ful, we face the challenge of building a secondary school of equal quality to ensure that our students can continue with their education. To that end, 25% of the proceeds for this book will be used to help pay for the construction and operation of our new school.

If you would like to learn more about our work in St. Marc, Haiti please visit our website at:

www.mortelfoundation.org

Breinigsville, PA USA
18 October 2009

225991BV00001B/2/P